LOVE. LIFE. DEATH. FREEDOM.

love.
life.
death.
freedom.

a memoir of my journey to
transformation and happiness

*Karolina
Magdalena*

Visit the author's website at www.moleculeofhappiness.com.

Visit the author's social media
to see the continuation of the story:
@moleculeofhappiness.

Love. Life. Death. Freedom.
a memoir of my journey to transformation and happiness

Written and published by Karolina Magdalena.

Finalized in Dominical, Costa Rica.

Cover illustration and design by Holly Dunn.
Internal illustration by Madli Silm.
Interior design by Euan Monaghan.

Interior photos © by Karolina Magdalena.
All rights reserved.

ISBN (paperback color): 978-3-9824777-0-1
ISBN (paperback b/w): 978-3-9824777-2-5
ISBN (e-book): 978-3-9824777-1-8

First edition: 2022

Grandma,
Love is who you are.
Love is where you are.
Forever inside me.

To my grandmother Lucyna
who was always waiting to
welcome me back after my journey.

She still does but among the stars.

Based on a true story and the way I see the world.

Contents

*T*here was a time in my life when I always prioritized everything else over my happiness—my career, financial security, family, partners, friends, and everyone else's needs and expectations. I would probably still be living that way today if it hadn't been for a dream I had one night that completely changed the course of my life.

I was thriving in a successful career, expanding my life through work projects that took me all over the world, and growing my savings account while spending countless hours perfecting deliverables that I prioritized over sleep. My romantic life wasn't fulfilling, but I called it stable. I didn't give up on love; I just put it on hold, believing that my heart could wait while the deadlines, buying an apartment, and taking care of those around me shouldn't. The apartment was perfect: well-decorated rooms full of designer furniture, a fully equipped kitchen, a comfortable mattress on my king-size bed, a wardrobe full of brand-new clothes—everything I needed in my so-called home. I also perceived that caring about others more than myself was a sign of a good heart, so I would never dare to question doing that, even when it became too much. "Look at you; your life is so impressive," people would say. "You were born in a small town without promising prospects, and you managed to make your way to all this." The things they admired made me feel unhappy and trapped. Yet I believed them as I was not able to listen to and understand my own heart.

Then that one weird, life-changing moment came—I fell asleep at midnight from exhaustion during a business trip in

Argentina and dreamed about a book. I saw the title, my name listed as the author, and the last sentence. *How weird,* was my first thought after I woke up. I continued living the same life, except with a strange feeling that kept nagging at me—a feeling that seemed to be my heart's way of telling me, "Go and write it."

After six months of the same words circulating in my mind, I'd had enough. I decided I finally wanted to be important to myself and follow what I felt, even if it meant going away from the perfect life to get closer to my confused heart. I decided to travel and dedicate myself to writing the book I had dreamed about. It seemed like the most unreasonable thing I had ever done, yet I needed to do it. Back then, I didn't yet understand how traveling to learn about love, life, death, and freedom could help me discover who I truly was and who I wanted to become. Now I know, and I would like to share the process of my self-discovery with you in hopes that it will encourage and help you connect with your own heart.

My journey took me to Nepal, India, Poland, Kyrgyzstan, the Philippines, Mexico, and Guatemala. The four big forces I met along the way–Love, Life, Death, and Freedom—taught me how to discover myself and look for my happiness. These forces take human form in this book, traveling with me and becoming my truest friends.

I welcome you to start the journey with me, and one day I hope to meet you somewhere in the world, happy and with your heart completely visible.

With love,
Karolina

The Beginning

The Warrior and The Healer

"When your opponent tries to hit you, your strength doesn't matter, only the clarity of your mind," my father, who taught martial arts, said to me right before his student launched a punch toward him.

The student's sharp exhale seemed to echo among the conifers at the top of the mountain, where we practiced martial arts every spring. I kept looking up at my father. His head of dark blonde hair covered my entire sky. In the shadow of a giant seemed to be the safest place to learn and grow. My father blocked the punch with the palm of his right hand and then grabbed his opponent's arm, twisted his body, and gracefully threw him over his shoulder to the ground. I scurried back with my little feet, worried that the heavy crash would cause an earthquake. My father placed his large hand on my shoulder.

"Don't be afraid. The mountains will always stand still. Their stillness will bring you clarity when you need it. Come back to them whenever any weakness obscures your way," he said, then turned around to lead his students down the mountain.

My father dedicated his life to something extraordinary—mastering and teaching martial arts in a place far away from its

Asian origins. He followed two Polish brothers who learned the practice by trying movements by themselves, getting inspiration from animal behaviors, reading the few available books from the pre-war period, and practicing the art of combat with foreign soldiers stationed in Poland. Even if Chinese traditions remained mysterious and unreachable, the brothers and their students incorporated the Christian values they were familiar with into everything they learned about martial arts. That fusion of two different cultures paved the way for martial arts as a physical and mental practice, which connected practitioners with their personal strength in a country where fighting was associated mostly with war.

"Every great warrior must master the art of combat as well as the art of healing," my father said one evening before I fell asleep. His goodnight stories filled my bedroom. Sometimes my mother's silhouette appeared at the door, shining with her short blonde hair and silver nails, perfectly matching her tunic-style shirt. She loved listening to him as well, even if combat wasn't her thing. She was his other half, the master of healing and the calm he always wanted to find. Surrounded by medical books full of pencil notes, healthy recipes cut out from magazines, and colorful mandala paintings she'd done herself, my mother was constantly discovering the ingredients of healing all around her. She treated the sick, tired, and hopeless. She healed them not only with her craft but also with the unconditional love from her soul.

"Healing is also a fight, but one you win with your heart," the Healer said to me while I was sitting on her lap one afternoon right before the Warrior came back home for lunch. Then she smiled, knowing that one day I would try to learn and understand it too. "Our biggest creation is and always will be our family," the Healer said to the Warrior as they sat together at the round, pine kitchen table for the first time after weeks of barely seeing each other. She was right; it was the only thing that kept them both powerful and safe.

"I have to go to work," he replied, avoiding looking into her eyes. The Warrior ate quickly, stood up from the table, grabbed his black duffel bag, walked downstairs, and got into his new, shining, dark blue Audi. "I will be back in a few days," he said indifferently before closing the door behind him.

The martial art academy was expanding to the entire country, and his new private security company was bringing him a fortune.

"Dad, are we going to the mountains?" I asked after he came back from his long business trip, knowing that only clarity could save my Warrior.

"I can't. I have to work," he answered, wanting more of everything but less of us.

I was eight years old. My heart, my life, and my mountains were shaking, even if the Warrior told me that they never would.

The Healer was crying in the living room, now empty of her books and recipes. She sat helplessly on the cold floor, a picture in her hand. It was of them madly in love, looking into each other's blue eyes and dancing during their wedding anniversary on New Year's Eve. She tore the picture into two so that nothing connected them anymore.

I touched her shoulder with my skinny hand, but she couldn't look at me. The Healer was hurt. The Warrior was gone.

If only I knew the way to my mountains, I thought to myself, scared and angry, as I sat on the floor next to her.

"Please don't cry," I said to my mom. And in my heart, I vowed to protect and fight for everything we had left, everything my father had left behind.

She sighed, wiped her tears, and smiled. "My brave child."

The Clock of Dreams

The old-fashioned clock hanging on my bedroom wall sometimes stopped for no reason. It was unnerving. I wasn't afraid of ghosts but of not having enough time to grow up and dream like a child. Facing the Warrior as an opponent scared me too. He met a new, young love and agreed to burn his old kingdom upon her wish to forget the past and begin their dreamlike life together. With madness in his blue eyes and knowing that we didn't have any source of income, he intended to take everything away from us—our home, food, education, and future—despite his fortune. It was the first time I learned something important, not from my Warrior, but because of him: *People aren't born strong and brave. They must decide to live and act with courage and constantly choose that path from one moment to the next.*

Tick-tock, tick-tock, dong! The little clock in my room suddenly started to work again. The time had come for me to make my decision to live bravely.

At seventeen, I grabbed the Healer's hand and led her into the courtroom. After nine years of constant battles, I faced the Warrior as his equal, armed with my file of papers. No longer his student, I had become my own master. Based on long months of preparation, I presented the facts and evidence as calmly and clearly as I could, and the judge ruled in our favor, securing our right to the apartment and alimony for food and education. The Warrior and the Healer remained silent while my greatest strength was born in fury.

"My brave child," the Healer said, looking at me with pride but also with a bit of worry. Even if I became the strongest, she still wanted me to dream like a child.

"There is an old and famous clock tower in London with a massive bell called Big Ben," my favorite teacher said during an English class one day, pointing at the picture in our schoolbook. "The bell's sound is present in the lives of millions every day, and its silence marks the saddest moments in British history."

Even before my teacher finished her story, I knew that I wanted to hear its powerful chime. One of the legends described in my schoolbook said that if Big Ben ever struck thirteen times instead of twelve, the lion statues in Trafalgar Squares would come to life. Legends don't need to be logical. Dreams don't need to be justified or even possible. They are my heart's way of teaching me how to be strong enough to venture out and change my life. The school bell rang. My time to dream had come.

Believing in the impossible wasn't easy. I lived in a small industrial town in Southern Poland where most people were content with a calm life without any worries. Miners with dark-lined eyelids dreamed about coming home safely every day. Hockey players sliding on the ice dreamed of winning the golden cup, but their deepest wishes were to create homes they could always slide back into. Young girls like me wanted to find love and create homes of their own, too. Any wish to travel was too expensive, too wild, and too complicated for the likes of us; a calm life was supposed to make us all happy. Happiness, however, isn't one size fits all, and the standard life everyone else seemed to want never suited me. I was fascinated by the big world.

I couldn't gaze at white dresses and build four stable walls to keep me always safe. I wanted to go places, learn things, and see sights unimaginable to me in my small town. So I told myself I would at least try to look for happiness elsewhere, to dream of something different, even if the odds were against me. To make it possible, I worked countless hours as a waitress, a sales clerk, a manicurist, and a proofreader. I could become anyone for a chance to be somebody I wanted—someone who dared to dream and challenge the impossible.

I did everything I could, but it wasn't enough. Still, it didn't hurt as much as not trying at all. Even if it was clear that I wasn't going to earn enough money to go to London and make my first dream happen, I continued working after school and counted on my luck. Tiredness and longing didn't make facing the impossible any easier, but for the first time, the striving made me feel that I was important to myself. My dreams and I were worth hanging on to for just a moment longer.

Tick-tock, tick-tock, dong! The old clock on my wall reminded me of my friend coming over soon. Anna opened the door without knocking, entered my room, and made herself comfortable on my blue sofa.

"You are so stubborn," she said to me, looking at the old clock I refused to throw away even though it no longer ran right. "It is hard to ignore that loud, ugly clock, but I have something more important to tell you today." Her conspiratorial tone made me curious. "In a few months, I will join my boyfriend in London to work for a while. Will you come with me?" Anna asked calmly, even though she knew we were moments away from jumping and shrieking together in excitement.

"Yes, absolutely!" I cried with joyful tears in my eyes as if her question had been the proposal most girls in my town dreamed of. In a way, it was a similar proposal for me: I was making the biggest commitment to myself, and despite my young age, I was ready to honor it for the rest of my life.

Ding, ding, ding! The airport bell announced the gate opening for my flight to London. Against all odds, I was leaving the old, ugly clock behind to make my first dream a reality. It was a powerful feeling to know that I would remember the next *dong, dong, dong* forever.

The Door to Love

I couldn't see the sky at all while looking up at the Big Ben tower. It covered my entire world, even though I felt much taller than ever before. *Dong, dong, dong,* the bell rang, and my heartbeat fell into sync with the sound. Its rhythm dissolved any memory of tiredness after making many efforts and softened the shock of the impossible. I stood before the clock tower, overwhelmed, and after a couple of minutes of my neck growing weary from craning upward, I looked down at my feet. They weren't small anymore. I was growing into a giant myself and starting to feel powerful even away from the mountains and outside of someone's shadow.

Big Ben wasn't just a dream or a bell inside a clock tower. It was a symbol of the opportunities I was creating for myself for a future that otherwise would be out of my reach. Long shifts in factories and hotels had exposed me to the big, wild world in which luck didn't matter, only survival and hard work. Using the money I'd saved while working abroad, I moved back to Poland to start studying law in the capital city, Warsaw. The legal profession wasn't my favorite form of combat, but it seemed to keep me and my family the safest, away from those who could hurt us, and with sufficient funds to never have to rely on anyone again.

My younger sister, or the Hummingbird as I called her, came to visit me regularly. Her way of being was different from mine—she was joyful, playful, spontaneous, and light. She was very tall and feminine, and her long blonde hair was always perfectly styled. She loved wearing and surrounding herself with colors. Her cheerful personality immediately attracted any person who came close to her—new lovers, friends, even strangers. Her heart was soft and always dangerously open, which made it easily breakable but also more accepting and forgiving than most. It was more eager to love.

"I'm proud of you, Sister. At the age of twenty, you're busy working seven days a week on your projects and studying long hours every night. But don't you feel you're missing something?" the Hummingbird asked right before we entered my apartment.

I held the key unnecessarily long in the door lock and didn't turn around to answer.

"Not really," I said, opening the door and letting her pass first. "Are you hungry?" I asked, hoping she wouldn't continue the topic.

"Always!" She smiled joyfully and walked toward the kitchen. "You can't ignore your heart and love life, you know," she persisted before taking the first bite of her cheese sandwich that she still had in her bag from the train ride.

"I don't know how to deal with it," I mumbled when preparing tea.

"Start by going out there and figuring out what love isn't about. It's still better than not trying at all—your words." She winked at me, opened the fridge, and closed it again with disappointment. "Let's go out for dinner!" she said. She always welcomed any excuse to enjoy life to the fullest.

I do miss the world, I thought to myself while sitting at my desk with a dozen massive books surrounding me later that night. I grew restless, and my bravery turned into a constant curiosity that made me feel like a child in the middle of my serious and ambitious life. The prospect of venturing out into the unknown fascinated me more than any achievements and a clearly defined future.

"I want to go abroad for exchange studies," I shared my new plan with the Hummingbird over the phone for the first time since she had visited me.

"You miss the world," she said, unsurprised. She knew me well. "Where will you go?" she asked.

"Finland," I answered.

"It's cold there!" she said and kept listening.

"It fits to my heart," I said and laughed.

She sighed, and I was almost sure she rolled her eyes.

She taught me how to want things joyfully like a child—spontaneously, unreasonably, and without a big plan. I sensed with excitement that something was about to change my entire life.

I moved to Finland a few months later during summer. It was surprisingly warm, and the sun shone until midnight. I arrived in a small student town, Turku, and unpacked my suitcase in a small dorm room furnished with a simple white bed, a wardrobe, and a bookshelf. The dorm had common bathing areas and rooms for entertainment and studying. The front yard was packed with bicycles, which students used all year round, even in winter. The dorm was surrounded by a never-ending forest.

It's simple. You got this, I thought to myself at the end of my first day as I fell asleep with the sunshine on my face.

By the second day, I had already bought my own bicycle, which its previous owner named 'Dragon.' I wasn't sure if we would both survive the upcoming winter as hand-me-down dragons and girls with cold feet weren't made for ice, but I didn't expect any problems when riding to the university on summer days.

I arrived for my first Finnish language class covered in sweat and dirt after taking an unnecessary and difficult shortcut. A classmate opened the door for me. I looked at his large feet first, then up his tall body to his muscular arms, full lips, radiant smile, blue eyes, and dark blonde hair. He smelled like tangerines. It couldn't be his perfume, though. Too feminine.

Big trouble, I thought to myself as I passed him quickly and headed toward the last row in the classroom. He followed me, sat next to me, and introduced himself as Michael.

Two weeks later, the smell of tangerines on him was gone. He only smelled of baked chestnuts now, which we had loved to eat since our first date. My feet were warm for the first time during winter. I was happily in love.

Soon winter was gone. Michael graduated and decided to move to Germany for work. Closing my thin door after him was difficult. I tossed stones on lakes. I couldn't accept their stillness. I listened to sad songs in forests. I couldn't stand their silence.

"Damn you, always change everything!" I shouted angrily at our favorite river, which kept us moving, even if I didn't want it to.

Nature listened patiently but didn't respond. My life was meant to go this way.

After one year of living in Finland, I finished my exchange program. I continued my education with a legal traineeship in Limassol, Cyprus—a remote paradise island with dreamy sea views. I arrived there to a white house surrounded by tangerine trees. I smiled.

"Is it love or not?" the Hummingbird asked over the phone.

"I don't know yet," I answered shortly.

"Why did you choose to be far away?" she asked.

"Because it is easier to forget than to beg someone to stay," I said confidently, even though I felt like a coward inside.

"Don't work too much. It doesn't help. Okay?" she asked her last question with care.

"I will be fine. I will keep trying to learn how to love, I swear," I said. I was sure that she was proud of me even from far away.

Never-ending sunshine, breakfast ready on my desk every morning, the sea view from the office, sunsets on the beach, and fruity cocktails after delicious Greek-style dinners—being alone in a faraway place wasn't as bad as some people say. But it wasn't where I wanted to be.

"Risking and leaving everything only for a chance to love?" I questioned myself in disbelief. "This is madness. You're so compulsive!" I continued to berate myself while packing my suitcase.

I smiled at the tangerine trees one last time before leaving on a flight to Germany.

Gone were the citrus trees, and in their place stood oaks and weeping willows. The Greek music was drowned out by the city noise. I wasn't walking barefoot on the beach anymore but running through the busy street crowded with luxury cars toward Michael's apartment. His heavy dark brown door was made of steel and frosted glass. I stood in front of it for a moment before ringing the bell. *Here I'm brave in the most fragile way,* I thought to myself. I blinked nervously, and suddenly his giant arms were around me.

"Welcome home, darling," he affectionately kissed the top of my head, and I closed my eyes.

The first kiss. The first dinner. The first laundry. The same breakfast. The same shower. The same keys. Home. "Could love be that simple?" I asked myself every morning. We traveled. We laughed. We met each other's families. Soon I found a job, started to speak German, and learned to cook better. After being lost in the world, I had come home.

One year later, our postbox was full of postcards that smelled like tangerines. I trusted him fully. Never mind.

He hated his job and the city which I moved to for him. I was there to make it better. Never mind.

He didn't like when I looked too pretty. I was still myself in my gray clothes. Never mind.

I ignored my heart and the hurt inside it. Never mind.

"I don't love you, and I don't know why," I said to Michael over the stove as we cooked our last dinner together.

"What did you say?" he angrily frowned.

I repeated it and added, "I am sorry."

"Your heart is empty, incapable of love, and always closed. You have two hours to pack up and move out!" he raised his voice and left the apartment for a walk.

It wasn't love, and maybe one day I would understand why. But for now, I closed the outer steel door, marking the beginning and end of our trying.

I didn't have anywhere to go. Germany, not Michael anymore, became my home. After one long month of wandering between the houses of strangers, I opened a scratched white door to a small and dark apartment. I slid down the wall, sat on the floor, and cried from the deepest darkest hole in my stomach. Somebody sat down beside me. I thought I was alone, but this person didn't scare me. Her hazel eyes were surrounded by long ginger curls and light brown freckles. Her skin looked soft and delicate. Everything about her felt familiar. She wasn't real but the most confusing and comforting fantasy of my own heart. Her name was Love.

"Do you regret your decision after losing everything?" Love asked, scooting closer.

"No. It wasn't about winning or losing but trying," I answered, and she smiled.

"Stand up! Come on, stand up right now!" She gave me her hand to pull me up as if she were in a hurry for us to go somewhere.

"Not so fast, not so fast," I said, wanting Love to calm down. I stood without her help.

Two years passed by. I continued my habit of working a lot, even on Fridays. I often left the office late. One late night, Matteo, a mysterious colleague who sat on the same floor as me but didn't speak much, held the glass door for me as we were both leaving. I didn't know much about him. He came from the United States, loved Mexican food, and one day wanted to go back to his Italian roots in Sardinia. I liked his long brown hair and the fact that he wasn't as tall as the giants.

"Well then?" Love nudged me and raised her eyebrows.

"Would you like to grab some dinner? It's too late to cook," Matteo asked me before I could answer Love.

"What?" I asked, distracted.

"Let's go get something to eat." He grabbed my hand and didn't wait for an answer.

After a short tram ride, we stood together in front of my favorite restaurant, which he chose, though he didn't know it was my favorite yet.

"I'm not used to..." I took my hand away before entering a Spanish restaurant.

At dinner, we talked on and on.

"How is it possible that we didn't speak much before?" I asked him.

"Better late than never," he said. "But I should mention, I'm moving back to the United States in one week."

"What?!" Love and I said together and almost choked on our wine.

"Meet me tomorrow," Matteo suggested.

"No, you're leaving." I raised my hands as if to push the thought of him away.

"It doesn't make me less human," he said and smiled.

"These kinds of stories are not kind to my heart," I responded with a serious face.

Inside my head, I shouted, *It isn't love, it isn't. I'm sure that it isn't!*

He kissed me. I spent his last week with him, and we stayed together for another year while living on different continents.

"It's fine as long as you choose wisely," Love said before our first anniversary.

The ringing phone interrupted her.

It was Matteo. "I can't live without you. Would you move to the United States?" he asked without saying hi.

"I can't give up everything... I can't open the same door twice," I answered, my voice breaking.

"What if our story happens only once?" he kept trying.

"I can't."

Those two short words broke his heart.

"Are you okay?" Love placed her hand on my shoulder as I was lying on my bed afterward, looking at the ceiling without blinking.

"I will be," I forced myself to smile. Turning to her, I asked, "It wasn't love again, and yet you're still here. Why?"

"I don't live because of them but always within you," she replied and closed our scratched white door for the night.

The Beast

When I was a child, my grandmother would tell me before I fell asleep, "You have to cover your feet before sleeping because there is an evil red duck with horns that comes at night to eat children's toes."

This creature scared me sometimes, but my grandmother always emphasized that it would do me no harm if I kept my feet warm. Ever since, I'd known how to keep away the beasts that lurked in the night. All that changed one evening when, at the age of twenty-eight, I turned into a beast myself.

When the darkness came, my body started to shake. My feet became hairy, wide, flat, and heavy. I sprouted long, sharp claws that scratched the floor, making me lose my balance with every unsteady step. The heat wave inside me was moving from my monstrous feet toward my lungs, burning their surface like I'd swallowed a torch. Was it magic or maybe a curse? Whatever it was, it was still bearable until it reached my heart.

"Don't break!" I shouted when my heart started beating too fast for me to keep up.

"Don't stop!" I shouted when it was beating too slow to keep me alive.

"Don't give up!" I shouted at my entire body, hoping that my voice would break through the thick, white-snow fur which started to grow over my skin.

"Don't..." I whispered before falling to the floor, a heavy newborn beast.

"Help..." I wasted my last conscious breath on that meaningless sound which, even though uttered, couldn't be heard by anybody.

I opened my eyes in the hospital. Somebody had heard. Somebody had found me. I looked at the white ceiling, white walls, white windows, white bed sheets, white gown, white uniforms, and the white door. And that terrible white fur. For the first time, white was a scarier color than black.

The doctor came in with a group of his students to examine me.

"What is it, doctor?" I pointed at my legs.

"Erythema nodosum," he answered, and the red swollen bumps all over my legs received a noble Latin name. "The first symptom of an autoimmune disease," he added.

"What does it mean?" I asked, disoriented.

"Your body started to attack its own cells without any specific reason," he tried to explain.

"How can I stop it?" I asked as my panic grew. I tried to calm down but realized that my weak lungs couldn't take a deep breath anymore.

"Unfortunately, we can't. There is no reliable medication or procedure that will cure your condition." The doctor looked into my red eyes and closed his files.

I wanted to cry. I wanted to roar. I was trapped in the body of this hungry beast that modern medicine couldn't tame.

"Am I dying?" I asked the doctor directly with tears in my eyes.

"Let's hope for the best," he said and smiled politely.

"Let's hope I don't die," I said to myself out loud after he left the room.

Nights at the hospital were scary. Not because I felt lonely between those empty white walls or uncomfortable in a bed somebody could have died in before me. Beasts don't feel any of that. They only want to survive and wake up in the morning like all the rest of us. I was waiting long hours, constantly fearful, as if something was hunting me, and then fell asleep, but only from exhaustion. When I finally closed my tired eyes, a woman came, sat on the edge of my bed, and put her cold hand on my burning forehead. Her touch woke me.

"Am I hallucinating?" I asked as I looked into her pearl eyes, which were visible through the darkness. "Who are you?" I looked at her long black hair, which covered most of her ivory embroidered dress, but I couldn't recognize her at all.

She moved her hand to my belly with a touch that felt like the caress of a caring mother.

"Mom?" I asked. She didn't look like the Healer, but I wasn't thinking clearly. I moved my fingers over her soft but cold hands from her knuckles to her wrist. It wasn't her. "You must be..." I said and couldn't believe it.

"Death," she finished and covered my feet with the blanket.

Even if I was still overwhelmed by her presence, I fell asleep like a cub.

The next day Matteo called me after sending me flowers. "How are you feeling?" he asked.

"Lonely and scared for the first time in my life," I answered with a shaking voice. I was dying just when I was beginning to learn how to love.

Even if I'd left him and insisted that sick warriors should

heal by themselves, deep inside, I'd hoped that he would come and love me unconditionally, sickness or not.

But he didn't. He repeated two sentences that had the power of a spell in my life, always ending something important: "I can't. I have to work."

After a week in the hospital, I had to leave as the doctors couldn't do anything more. I went home, feeling like I couldn't either. *Breathe in, breathe out, take a step forward. Breathe in, breathe out, take another step. Breathe in, breathe out, keep your tired eyes open. Breathe in, breathe out, rest. Stay strong… stay strong.* Finally, I arrived. Love opened the door to my apartment. Death let me pass first, then followed me in and kissed Love on the cheek.

"The fur!" Love was speechless for a moment as she touched my face with her delicate fingers. "You need a warm bath." She slowly led me to the bathroom, helped me to get into the bathtub, and held my eyelids open so that I wouldn't fall asleep and drown.

"Home," I whispered to myself and hugged my naked knees until the water got cold.

The first bath I remember was with my grandma. I was five years old. She prepared the warm water with lots of lavender foam and hid a yellow rubber ducky in it. When I suddenly discovered the ducky while splashing among bubbles, I moved my feet away from it and looked at my grandma with scared eyes. She laughed. "Sometimes ducks aren't as scary as they seem to be. You're alright, honey." With time, I allowed the yellow ducky to float closer and closer until I was brave enough to squeeze it and laugh at the squeaking sound it made. My grandma was watching over me and smiling with pride.

"Everything is fine. It isn't as bad as it seems," I said to my grandma over the phone twenty-three years later, mindful to keep my voice calm so as not to worry her too much. But she knew everything. She always had, ever since the first time I heard her beating heart.

Lub-dub, lub-dub. When I said that I was fine without the Warrior in our lives, she hugged me.

Lub-dub, lub-dub. When I said that I didn't want to talk about my teenage insecurities, she stayed quiet and listened anyway.

Lub-dub, lub-dub. When somebody broke my heart, she switched the channel whenever a romantic movie started and served another piece of cheesecake to make me feel better.

Lub-dub, lub-dub. When I studied and worked until late at night, she didn't ask me to stop but called me more often so that I could rest for a moment.

Lub-dub, lub-dub. "I love you," she said each time we spoke, always giving name to the *lub-dub* beat of her heart.

She taught me that loving and caring about me was easy—that I was lovable and important. Even if knowing that wasn't enough to heal me, it made me feel like fighting for myself, or at least trying to, was worth it.

When I hung up the phone, nothing was fine anymore. I couldn't eat. My shaking furry hands were too clumsy. I couldn't look at my body. It was too pale to look alive. I couldn't exercise or walk. Even as my muscles shrank and I grew smaller, this body of the white bear felt too heavy. I couldn't feel. My beating heart was too faint to still be human.

"You're sick! You're weak! You failed me!" I was angry at my own body. "I didn't do anything wrong! I ate healthy, exercised, and took breaks, but it was never enough. Why are you doing this to me?"

Dying felt like breaking up with myself. I blamed my body for its weakness, yet I wasn't without fault myself. Working too much, sleeping too little, not taking enough time to think about who and what was good for me, not resting when I felt exhausted, only when my schedule allowed. Now my only choice was to sleep and hope it wouldn't last forever.

"Wake up! Warriors never give up, even when dying!" Death pulled the blanket from me and opened the curtains, letting in the morning sun.

"You were supposed to wait for me," I said to her, surprised.

"I can't just sit and watch you become like those cowards who left you behind," she said in an annoyed voice while opening my wardrobe to find fresh clothes.

"Excuse me?" I asked, annoyed.

Her response was to throw a white t-shirt onto my face.

"For heaven's sake, love and fight for your beast!" she shouted into my bedroom as if I'd offended her by giving up on myself. She was sometimes tired but never gave up on anybody.

I stood up. *Lub-dub. Lub-dub.* I knew that my destiny wasn't ruled by the doctor's verdict but by my still-beating heart. This was to be my most important fight.

I rolled out a yoga mat on the floor. *Let's start slowly,* I thought to myself as I began gently stretching my body. Even if there was no medication known to heal my beast, I chose the world's most famous exercise poses as my first powerful step toward fighting for my health.

My business phone rang. "Ignore it. For now, just focus," I said loudly, making myself the priority.

If you slow down your career now, who are you going to become? My mind protested, but I didn't care.

I walked toward the kitchen to prepare a warm and nourishing porridge. "Eat, I must eat," I reminded myself, trying to break my body's resistance with every lift of my spoon.

"I know that you're trying, but I can't," my body responded, but I wasn't angry.

"I need to understand my body better." I opened a book about traditional Chinese medicine as I lay on the sofa and sipped a tea of ginger and cinnamon, which got cold before I finished reading the first ten pages. "No worries, take your time. I will make a new cup," I silenced my body and mind before either of them could start complaining.

I decided I needed to clear my mind and my life. I went through my phone and deleted all the toxic people who had already stayed in my life for far too long.

"How are you going to live without them?" my mind asked, still ignoring my efforts to keep us alive.

"Damn you!" I said to my body and mind. "No matter how much you reject my efforts, I will always love you and fight for us. Until the very end, I will never give up and leave you behind."

After a full year of tirelessly trying to heal my body, I burst into tears. I felt that no matter what I did, I could neither live nor die.

Lub-dub. Lub-dub. I will always love you. My monstrous heart slowly beat as it unexpectedly woke from hibernation.

"It's the first heartbeat of mature love," Death said to me with a hopeful smile.

"Mature because it happened slowly and gradually?" I asked.

Death paused for a moment in front of me, took both of my hands into hers, looked into my blue eyes, and said, *"No. Because you stopped expecting others to teach you how to unconditionally love yourself. Now you feel it in your own heart instead."*

I could feel her cold hands not through the pads of my snow-white paws but on bare human skin tanned by the summer sun. The beast was gone. From that moment, I knew that I was going to love and be loved, regardless of how other hearts felt or what path I wanted to or had to take.

The Broken Flowerpot

One morning while opening the window to my grandmother's bedroom, I accidentally knocked over her favorite vintage blue flowerpot holding the white-pink orchid from a windowsill.

Oh no! She will kill me for sure, I panicked. Her beloved carpet, which was older than me, was now full of soil and the broken pieces of her treasured pot. I started to collect the shards when she walked into the room.

"Grandma, I'm sorry," I looked at her from the floor, hoping that I wouldn't make her sad.

Her face went pale for a moment, but then she smiled.

"It doesn't matter. It was pretty, but that orchid outgrew it already ten years ago before you were even born. We will repot it now, and it will bloom more in the fall," she said in a soft voice, ignoring my clumsiness and her precious loss.

I smiled. She loved me above all.

My life in Germany before my illness was like a pretty pot. Inside, I'd planted a successful international career in a big corporation, a bank account full of savings that kept me secure, vacations to unforgettable destinations, a bucket list full of ideas, friendships that brought me joy, potential husbands ready to build a family house with the view of the entire valley and my apartment in the city center, which kept me connected to all the cosmopolitan luxuries and entertainment money could buy. Nothing felt safer than living in that solid pot I'd settled in for all the years to come.

So I put my high heels back on and returned to work. The shoes fit, but they hurt my feet like never before. I checked my bank account every day to remember why I was forcing myself to wear them. When I finally took them off during my all-inclusive vacation, I felt bad that I was happy only during breaks from my daily life. And when I got back home, the same people who used to make me feel joyful were too busy to notice that I had been mostly alone for quite a while. My bucket list had dwindled down to a single item: to stay alive. Marriage wasn't on that list, so even if any suitors presented themselves, I didn't want the fancy houses they dreamed of and offered. There was no lake, no mountains, no sea—only the forest, which became my peaceful place where I ran away from having to accept that I had outgrown my pretty pot as well. This forest and my comfortable life weren't enough for my heart.

"What's wrong, my girl?" my grandma asked over the phone two years after I had won my second chance at a long life.

"I have worked so hard for everything I have right now, and yet I don't feel happy. I don't feel it at all, and pretending to be happy doesn't feel much different from slowly dying," I said to her, feeling ungrateful and sad.

"Then change it. You can always change," she replied.

Her answer surprised me, as I thought that it was my successful life that made her proud.

"But people don't just throw away their good lives without a reason. I have nothing to escape from or complain about. I don't have dreams that can't wait. I don't even have a love story to follow," I said and took a sip of herbal tea she sent me via post every month to make sure that I was taking care of myself.

"Having a choice is the most powerful reason for any change," she said.

"Yes, but you only changed the pot for the orchid when I broke it, even if it was too small a long time ago," I answered.

"Because my happiness isn't about that flower but about you. I would have changed it long before if that's what was needed to keep you smiling," she said, and the echo of her *lub-dub* sound reached my heart again.

"You change so things will change with you. Such is life," Death added when I hung up the phone.

"Let's make dinner," I said to her without any other comment.

"I'll be bringing a friend, if you don't mind," Death said as she opened the fridge.

She knew everyone, so I wasn't surprised that she wanted to socialize.

Love arrived with a shopping bag full of ripe tomatoes, basil, ginger, pasta, and French red wine. Death started to cut the onions and garlic while Love decided to start with a glass of wine. Somebody knocked on the door.

"It must be your friend," I said to Death and stopped cutting tomatoes for a moment. I opened the door to find a strange lady with sapphire blue eyes, distinct high cheekbones, and shoulder-long, honey blonde hair. She kissed me on the cheek in greeting. She looked very classy, almost Hollywood-glamourous, in her simple black dress.

I looked at my white t-shirt with red tomato stains on it and then said to her, "You look beautiful."

"Thank you for the warm welcome," she said with a laugh.

I led her to the kitchen without introducing myself. Love had taken over the tomatoes and had them in olive oil in a frying pan, slowly simmering into sauce.

"Stop stealing my sauce with your fingers!" she scolded Death, but Death only shrugged her shoulders with a smile that promised nothing.

I put pasta into a big pot with boiling water and drifted away with my thoughts.

I can't give up on the life I worked so hard for, the life that keeps me safe and stable, I thought as I made circles with a spoon in the boiling water.

The glamorous newcomer came closer, took the spoon from me, and said, "Your pretty pot is already broken. Don't feel bad about it. Unhappiness isn't there to break you but to break the silence of your waiting heart. It wants you to grow. It wants you to go."

I was shocked that she had read my mind.

"You are one of them, aren't you?" I had figured as much.

She smiled and switched off the stove below the boiling pot.

"Pasta is ready!" she called to Death and Love, who took it as their cue to finish seasoning the tomato sauce. Then she turned to me and flashed her perfectly white, photogenic smile. "Yes, my name is Life."

"Three of you! Crazy!" I said as I fumbled as to drain the pasta through a colander in the sink.

"Stop acting weird. It's all okay." Death laughed and nudged me on her way to put a dirty frying pan into the sink.

Love mixed pasta with the tomato ginger sauce in a bowl, put portions on the plates, and decorated them with fresh basil.

"We haven't made this tomato ginger recipe before, have we?" Death asked, bringing cutlery to the table.

"Well, I got it from her grandma. I felt like trying something new to celebrate her decision," Love answered.

"What decision?" Death asked back.

Life set a big shiny wine glass next to each plate, and Love poured her favorite French red wine.

"She decided to give up everything again, but this time it will be for herself," Love said and looked at me, expecting me to say more.

"I want to pack my backpack and start a journey without a plan, only to explore, understand more, and find what makes me truly happy," I said.

Death and Life looked at each other and joyfully smiled. Love raised her glass to make a toast and looked at Death as she opened her mouth to speak.

"To all the broken flowerpots, we choose not to mourn but to celebrate with a glass of good wine," Death started.

"To embracing changes and choosing ourselves over all the things we thought should define us," Life continued.

"And last but not least, to our stubborn hearts which can't keep us safe but that are always ready to risk everything to make us happy," Love added before clinking her glass with everybody and inviting us to eat this delicious new pasta recipe.

"The journey begins." Death finished her wine and tapped the side of her empty glass, making the familiar *dong, dong, dong* of change ringing in.

Nepal

APRIL 2019

Mount Foreverest

"Ouch!" A hungry stray bit Death on her skinny hand as we walked down the street after arriving in Kathmandu. "Sorry. What did you say?" she asked me as she reached down to pet the brown dog, which had suddenly become peaceful and obedient.

"What is the most important thing when starting a new life?" I asked her again.

"Not to carry your heavy past around with you," she answered.

The dog suddenly sniffed her, recognized her smell, and kept walking by her side.

"Am I healthy, or will my disease come back?" I'd asked myself this question every day for two years. Even after winning the fight for my life, I never put down my heavy sword. The disease had irreversibly weakened my lungs, and when I felt tired, it always brought back the fear of dying. I had to stay vigilant. Fear can be as powerful as love—it followed me and distorted how I saw myself and the world. Both exist to teach me about letting go. I wanted to let go and feel love again, not to let fear prevail.

Death brought me to Nepal to look for clarity and closure close to the peak of the highest mountains in the world. She followed what the Warrior had taught me and chose the only place which still united us, even though we were now worlds apart.

Walking one hundred and thirty kilometers over twelve days with the significantly dropping oxygen level wasn't prescribed as my aftercare. But my definition of self-care was different. I had to follow what my heart needed.

After a few strong heartbeats, I boarded a small plane to Lukla. This flight had become infamous for crashes that had killed many people. Death was sitting comfortably and watching the view from a small window, hoping to remain unnoticed. I was impressed with her—her ivory embroidered dress combined with sturdy brown hiking shoes made her look extraordinary.

We landed safely and looked around at the mountains covered by a dense forest of green trees surrounding us, blocking any way out. *I don't know how I'll walk so far, but I will try,* I thought to myself, believing that my strong will could soften the impossible again.

I started the hike with Death by my side. Love and Life were walking ahead of us, sipping water from their matching red steel bottles, chatting joyfully as if this were a simple walk in the park.

"Forever begins now," Death smiled at me and touched the sword on my back. "Let's go up!" she said enthusiastically and scared away all the birds in the surrounding trees.

I walked higher, step by step, one breath after another. Even if I couldn't keep up with Love, Life, and the other hikers, I felt strong. Death lagged behind with me, patiently reminding me to drink water and tighten my shoelaces right before the steepest hills. I couldn't pretend to her that the walk was easy. It wasn't. As I climbed uphill for hours with aching muscles and under the unmerciful sun, my short breaths reminded me of my limitations. Yet all the physical strain couldn't distract me from the beauty of everything around me—everything which, in contradiction to Death and my past, was lush, green, and alive.

I walked among mountain giants and Himalayan blue pines and followed the rushing turquoise-white waters of the Dudh Kosi River on the way to Namche Bazaar. I laughed a lot with the trek guides and my hiking companions and enjoyed eating simple food and falling asleep from exhaustion in wood and stone houses without showers. After three days of walking, the snowy mountain view became even more breathtaking when we approached the holy place of Tyangboche, where monks were powerfully chanting and playing ritual music in their simple but majestic monastery. The sound of their drums and bells penetrated me from my ears, through my heart, and down toward my feet. This feeling reminded me of the heat wave that had burned through my body at the beginning of my disease. But this was power of a different sort.

"No fear. No fear. No fear. You're alright," I repeated to myself while watching a chubby, bald monk rhythmically hitting his drum.

"Enough. It's done. We need to continue," Death nudged me. She always got annoyed whenever somebody thought that letting go required a lifetime, not only a mere moment.

We walked further and passed the swinging suspension bridge that stretched over the Imja Khola River. I looked to the side and found our way was lined with thousands of colorful Mani stones carved with the ancient Buddhist mantra 'Om mani padme hum.' The Dalai Lama had praised these words for their purifying power. After six days of walking and panting, we arrived at the traditional Sherpa village of Dingboche, where I was reminded once more that a simple life exposes what is truly important—to breathe, eat, and care for those you love, including yourself.

"It's impossibly hard, but I love it!" I said to sweaty Death before walking up another steep hill.

"Suffering is great," she answered with an ironic tone, bracing her hands on her hurting knees.

As we continued walking, the landscape was changing again. Trees and birds disappeared, but the sky wasn't silent. Helicopters flew overhead, evacuating people who had become dangerously exhausted and not able to adapt to the high altitude. Death, Love, Life, and I finally reached the last wood and stone house before the Mount Everest Base Camp and shivered the whole night in dirty clothes under smelly blankets.

The next day, the world turned into a different planet. The rocky landscape was raw, dry, and overwhelming. People weren't the same anymore. They couldn't eat, their steps grew heavy and slow, and their eyes looked vacant because of a burning fever.

"Why am I still strong, not getting sick from the high altitude like everyone else?" I asked Death.

"Because you have already been strong for quite a while," she answered and smiled like a caring mother.

For quite a while... it echoed in my mind.

"What did I need the mountains for?" I asked again.

"To stop living as a survivor, let go and become someone who laughs and enjoys everything that comes after," she said, pointing at Mount Everest peak, the tallest point on Earth.

I bowed my head and closed my eyes. We made it. My body and I not only survived but felt more alive than ever. Together, with joy, we lifted and finally set down our sword. Mount Everest and Death herself had united us forever.

Mount Everest Base Camp (5 364 m), Nepal. April 2019.

The Gate

"Stop it! You can't rob me! It's mine!" I tussled with a stubborn monkey as it kept pulling at my backpack with its wild strength.

Old cars rushed by right behind us, more dangerous and louder with their honking than any avalanche. The city's polluted air was even harder on the lungs than the limited oxygen atop Mount Everest. The sellers were chirping almost like birds, trying to find new homes for their wonders of the world. While everything around was distracting to my eyes and ears, my nose had a clear direction and focus: Nepali food. Traditional Dal Bhat consisting of rice, a lentil soup, and vegetable curry, had the irresistible power to slow down everything and everyone during mealtimes. When stomachs were full and tables empty, tourists and locals continued about their busy schedules and adventures. I followed the crowd to the main street of Thamel, where tourists always came to shop, grab coffees, and sit down in the floral Garden of Dreams to unwind.

"This way or that way?" I looked at the crowded main street and then a narrow side street, which was oddly quiet and calm.

I was making decisions less and less based on reason—these days, the unknown always won.

I turned down the narrow side street. The noise went down, and the dust started to reveal cracked buildings with walls supported by wood logs. Gone were the lively shops and restaurants, and the street became monotonous and ordinary, all gray concrete and red bricks.

"What an exciting unbeaten path, huh?" Life giggled, looking at me.

"Nobody appreciates your irony." I rolled my eyes.

Then just a few steps later, we both suddenly stopped, dumbfounded by the view in front of us.

"Is that a golden gate?!" Life exclaimed.

We looked at each other in disbelief.

We walked closer, passing a dark-skinned woman standing by the gate, leaning on her blue motorcycle. Her beautiful black, puffy, afro curls dressed in small braids on the top of her head momentarily distracted me from our discovery. Even though it was burning hot, she wore a black leather jacket over a yellow t-shirt. There was something unreal about her. She didn't seem to sweat at all. I could smell her jasmine scent, which made me feel peaceful and trusting.

Life didn't seem to be surprised by her presence. She smiled as we walked past her and confidently knocked on the gate as if it was the door to a good friend's house.

"Okay, let's see." I looked at the slowly opening gate.

"Come in, sister," a woman dressed in a white robe said in a comforting, almost hypnotizing voice.

I walked in, and she locked the gate behind me.

"My name is Rona," she said and led me to a big room with two red armchairs. She gestured me toward them.

I sat in one of them and touched it with my fingertips.

Oh my, it's all real, I thought to myself and kept looking at her without any movement.

The white-robed woman took the other chair, looked at me, and said, "Your soul shines at a point in the center of your forehead."

As she continued to speak, I learned that she was a member of Brahma Kumaris, a religious movement with a focus on the soul as the most important part of human identity. She told me about her international spiritual organization led by women, all of whom live in strict celibacy, even when married. Celibacy not only with regard to the purity of their bodies but also to their thoughts, words, and actions. It was essential to achieve their joint goal—to connect and stay connected with their god called the Supreme Soul.

While she spoke, I looked at her with fascination. Not because of what she said, but out of awe for the courage she had to walk through that gate and commit herself to a place, a set of beliefs, and a group of people for the rest of her life. For me, it was still easier to get lost far away in the world than to decide that I belonged somewhere or to someone. My journey was a chance to find my place, some bigger vision, or a person to whom I might commit. Only, I wasn't sure whether I could ever learn to attach myself and live in that way forever.

Rona took a little bag of cookies from a shelf behind her and gave them to me. "Let your soul enjoy simple things." She smiled warmly, like an aunt, despite her mystical appearance.

After three hours of conversation, we stood up from those uncomfortable red armchairs. Rona didn't show any sign of discomfort in her body. She loved her life with her entire soul. She led me back through the big empty hallway toward the gate. On the other side, the woman in a yellow t-shirt and black leather jacket was still there. I didn't understand why, and she didn't offer any explanation. But it didn't matter. I learned to accept the most unusual happenings on that day.

Three days later, I left Kathmandu and headed toward Lumbini, where, according to the Buddhist tradition, Siddhartha Gautama was born and started his path to liberation as Buddha. Over two thousand years later, my path was crossing his. His footprints couldn't be seen on the soil anymore, but he was present in the mind of many people in that country, not to mention the countless majestic monasteries and colorful temples that reminded everyone of his timeless heritage.

There is always a beginning, even for things that will last forever, I thought to myself when arriving at the Maya Devi Temple, where Buddha is said to have been born. The garden surrounding the white temple was decorated with colorful prayer flags that were moving with the wind, spreading silent blessings for happiness and prosperity. Twelve barefoot monks wearing orange robes were sitting by the giant age-old Bodhi tree and chanting spiritual scripts. One of them, who had unusually big ears, suddenly stood up and walked toward me.

"Why are you here so early?" he asked simply. Based on his calm expression, I couldn't tell whether it was a problem or not.

"I guess I like early mornings as much as new beginnings," I shrugged my shoulders and replied with the first thing that came to my mind.

He waved his hand toward the other monks, walked back, and made space for me on the little red carpet next to him. The other eleven monks watched me following him with a peaceful curiosity in their eyes.

I sat down slowly, looking at them one by one. The monk

with big ears took his own seat next to me and looked at the temple.

"You came here not to see but to understand," he said the statement slowly like he didn't expect an answer.

"Yes, that is what my journey is about," I quietly agreed and looked down at the ground.

"Don't have any expectations for your journey. The lack of need for things to be or happen in a certain way allows us to discover real freedom and what is best for us," he said. *"Freedom isn't about belonging or not belonging to places, visions, and people but knowing that you are complete regardless of what surrounds you, what you feel or think inside you, and who joins or leaves your path,"* he continued and lifted my chin to pull my gaze up from the ground.

I thought over his words again. My journey wasn't about finding happiness through belonging somewhere, to someone, or some bigger vision, but learning how to create happiness inside me regardless of what happened. I needed to belong to myself, not to the external world, to be truly free.

Suddenly, the monks stood up one by one.

"You know, my friend, we will go now. Even monks are hungry sometimes." With that, he bowed and headed toward the green gate with the others.

Unexpectedly, I smelled the scent of jasmine again. I turned around and couldn't believe my eyes. It was her again! The mysterious, dark-skinned woman whom I saw in Kathmandu was standing right in front of me.

"They're closing the gate soon. I'm sure that you don't want to get trapped here," she said and started to walk with me toward the gate.

Love, Life, and Death were waiting for me outside and had little orange flowers tucked behind their ears. The monks must have passed them by and made them like that color, too. They all smiled when they noticed the mysterious woman who waved at them.

"See you soon, my friends," she said to the group of us, then walked toward her motorcycle and drove away.

"Who was she? Is she one of you?" I asked Life, surprised that they all knew her.

"Didn't you recognize her?" she asked back.

"No," I shook my head.

"Her name is Freedom, and yes, she is one of us," Life answered, then took the orange flower from her ear and tucked it behind mine.

"Love, Life, Death, and Freedom." I sighed and looked at Love, Life, and Death, who were still standing next to the green gate. I turned around and smiled. I was ready to leave Lumbini and continue my journey, belonging only to my own heart.

Monks and I. Lumbini, Nepal. April 2019.

Magnolia

"What the hell?! You almost scared me to death!" shouted the girl who had opened the door to the orange house where I was staying near Phewa Lake in Pokhara. Her distracted eyes became scared when she nearly ran right into me.

"Really? To death?" Next to me, Death rolled her eyes with disapproval.

"Calm down," I said to the Korean-looking girl with porcelain skin, mystic tattoos, and panda ears fashioned from her shiny black hair.

"Please don't play with my weak heart like that," she said theatrically, keeping her hand with black nails pressed to her chest.

"It won't happen again, I promise," I said, placing my cold hand to my own heart in response.

"Magnolia," she introduced herself and shook my other hand as her breathing slowed down. "I need to go to work, to the tailor shop around the corner. Are we housemates now?" she asked, eyeing my packed bags.

I nodded.

"Let's meet later at the Juicery Café for a late lunch at four o'clock," she said. "It's right across the street."

"You're a tailor...?" I asked, surprised, silently accepting the invitation.

"I'm a fashion designer and painter. We're working on something big!" she answered and headed toward the tailor shop. "I will see you later."

"Artist—of course!" I said to Death, just before the Nepali lady of the house came to greet me. She was very short but spoke so loudly that neither her family nor international guests could ignore her importance.

I dropped my bags in my room and went for a walk. I went to the lake and watched a rainbow of yellow and red paragliders flying from the sky toward the water's surface, where blue boats were cruising. I didn't want to fly, but I loved being close to water. Discovering each unknown place was like a new beginning. There was nothing I was used to. I could learn anew what I liked and disliked—colors, places, music, food, and people. I didn't like the only five boring black t-shirts I'd packed anymore. The world was more joyful when it was full of colors, I decided. I didn't use headphones anymore while walking on the noisy street. I loved secretly stepping in time to the rhythm of Nepali folk, hip-hop, or modern pop music, which made any other street noise irrelevant. A simple bowl of lentils and rice tasted better than a pizza. I also started to like people who didn't and couldn't entirely understand my life. I knew that only they could teach me how to understand myself better through their different perspectives.

I checked the time. Five minutes to four? *Oh no! I will be late,* I thought and quickly walked back along the lake toward the Juicery Café. When I arrived, Magnolia was sitting in the backyard at a scratched wooden table with her pencil and notebook out with a drawing in it. Being late didn't matter. She kept drawing even when I sat next to her. I looked at the black tattoos decorating her pale skin and tried to connect them, to read their story.

Before I could make sense of them, she closed her notebook and, noticing me staring, sighed and said, "It's just a body."

"Just a body? What do you mean?" I wanted to know more.

"Let's order first." She waved at the waiter, who seemed to be her friend. "Green juice for us, please," she said with a smile.

"Yes, darling," he answered and looked at her with a spark in his eyes. There was something dark and attractive about her at the same time.

It was unfair to start our first long conversation with difficult questions, I felt.

"How was work today?" I decided to ask the most ordinary question instead.

"Good. We are ready with our clothing collection inspired by South Korean traditions, and soon we will be able to ship it worldwide." Magnolia sounded like a fashion guru even as she sat barefoot at our simple scratched table.

"Are you from South Korea?" I asked.

"Yes." She answered right before the heavy green juice glasses arrived on our wobbly table.

"Do you miss your country sometimes?" I asked.

"Do you miss any place where your life was dark?" she replied, taking a sip of her juice.

"Sure. There is always something to miss about those places because life is never entirely dark," I answered and took my first sip too.

"You are like sunshine. I like you," she placed her elbow on the table and put her chin on her hand.

"You mean my blonde hair." I winked at her and waved at the waiter to order the daily special—vegetarian smoked mushroom burgers.

"Back in South Korea, I learned how to be creative. My art

started there when my mother taught me how to paint canvas. But life was also brutal, and it forced me to look for creative ways to survive," she said and smiled at the waiter who was taking an order from the table next to us.

"Creative ways?" I asked, unsure if she meant something other than fashion.

"I sold my body to rich men as an escort." She gulped a big sip of her green juice. "Just to survive," she added after a moment. "But it seems that once you tell yourself that love doesn't matter, life will always show you that you were wrong." She looked directly into my eyes.

Love suddenly pulled a chair up to our table and carefully sat down.

"Life always does it. That's what friends are for," Love continued the conversation and took a sip from my green juice.

"I thought that it was healing or fun, but I was simply falling apart. My body became just a body. It felt empty, so I used it to continue living among people without love—drugs, sex orgies, and toxic relationships," she continued her story as the burgers arrived on our table. "It wasn't healing. Escaping from love never heals." She took the first bite of her burger, and a heavenly expression came over her face.

"You never wanted to have a break from connecting with people and rest from what burns you?" I asked.

"Hiding away from love in the darkness makes you comfortable and can become addictive too," she said.

I gulped, feeling my heart beating faster. "Sometimes it's good to hide and heal," I answered.

It is always possible to heal yourself alone, hiding away from those with whom you are supposed to share love. But it's more powerful to heal while trusting love and continuing to grow among others,"

Magnolia said, and I admired her for the strength she had after everything she went through.

Maybe we weren't much different after all. Trying always kept us going forward.

"Enough of hiding," I said to Love, even if we both knew that there was a lot to handle during my journey.

"Okay, it's risky but let's try," she replied.

I asked the waiter for the bill.

After we paid, I waited for Love to stand up first.

Magnolia stood next, passed the empty third chair, and randomly said, "Oh, I hadn't noticed that chair there before."

Love turned back, smiled over her shoulder as she led us toward the exit, and said, "Sometimes you don't notice, but I'm always here."

Footprints

The next morning, I heard someone's rushed steps right behind me. I turned to look as a man's voice called out.

"Hey! Wait! I know you!" the Dutch-accented voice interrupted my walk along the street toward the lake.

Magnolia was working at the tailor's again at that time. It was also impossible that I knew anyone else in this part of the world as I had never been to Asia before. I turned around and looked indifferently at the tall blonde man with blue eyes who suddenly stopped. His wide smile with a little gap between the front teeth reminded me of nobody, so I stood there with raised eyebrows.

"We were on the same connecting flight from Istanbul to Kathmandu," he said enthusiastically.

"That's great," I answered shortly.

"You're doing great with trying, honey," Freedom laughed.

"Nice wine-red lipstick," I looked at her and mentally retorted, ignoring her sarcastic mood.

"My name is Daan," the stranger said.

"Karolina," I answered and recalled him standing behind me at the boarding counter in Istanbul. Maybe he wasn't a crazy stranger after all. "It's so weird that Love isn't here with us. Where is she?" I asked Life in my mind.

"I don't know. Let her breathe," Life answered, putting on her glamorous light beige, wide-brimmed summer hat and sipping her mango lassi through a colorful metal straw.

"Talk to him; you only live once," Death added, wiping sweat from her forehead.

"I wouldn't be so sure about that, but go for it," Life looked at me from below her hat.

Death looked at her hat with disapproval, but Life didn't care at all.

"One life or many, follow what you feel right now," Freedom said quietly, taking a step toward me as if she didn't want the rest to hear.

"Where are you from, Daan?" I asked, starting our travel conversation in the most usual way.

"From the Netherlands, Rotterdam," he answered, and we started to walk together. "And you?"

"Poland. I will buy you a drink if you can pronounce my hometown." I laughed, and our conversation warmed up because, of course, he couldn't. "Are you here on vacation?" I asked, even if I could tell that he was a tourist.

"Yes. I want to do the Annapurna trek, visit a monastery to learn how to meditate, and go to the jungle in the Chitwan National Park," he said eagerly.

"Impressive plan," I answered as I looked along the side of the road for someone selling something to drink.

"Thanks. And you? What are your plans?" Daan asked curiously.

"I'm not sure if I have any. To find or create home," I said, and my eyes brightened when I spotted a mango lassi stand on our way.

"You want to learn how to meditate in a monastery... Would you rather be a monk or a warrior?" I asked, trying to find one thing which connected us.

"Definitely a monk," he answered. "And you?"

"Always a warrior." I smiled, and the taste of mango distracted me from our differences.

"It's getting late, and I need to pack for my trek tomorrow. Would you like to join me in my hotel room and continue our conversation?" he asked the million-dollar question.

I wasn't sure, but I liked going with the flow, so I nodded and followed him upstairs.

"Recently, somebody broke my heart," he mentioned even though I didn't ask.

"How?" I tried to avoid the uncomfortable silence.

"We were engaged. We bought a house. One day I was walking on the street and randomly met a beautiful and smart blonde woman. I immediately fell in love. That coincidence felt like destiny. I canceled my wedding for her, but she decided to stay with her partner. I risked everything for nothing."

I listened to him patiently from a chair as he moved about his room, picking up this and that.

"Destiny is for lazy people. Coincidence is an opportunity to connect, not to find love without effort and lessons," Freedom said from the armchair next to me.

"Hey, Freedom, maybe we shouldn't judge people too quickly," I answered.

She seemed to like my cheeky response.

"I will go now," I said and stood up from the armchair.

"Do you want to exchange numbers?" Daan asked.

"Here you go," I took a piece of paper from the table and wrote my number, then walked toward the door.

He kept the door open as I walked downstairs. I didn't look back, but it made me smile. He wasn't my warrior, but maybe monks were learning how to love despite differences, too.

The next day, Daan left for his five-day trek. Magnolia joined me for breakfast at the Juicery Café.

"You stopped hiding from men, didn't you?" she took a sip of her cappuccino after glimpsing my phone, which lay on our scratched tabletop.

"There was a strange coincidence which makes me wonder." I told her the story of my unexpected encounter with Daan. "He seems to be a good person, but I don't really feel it," I added.

I have tried to love bad people. I asked myself why I loved them. I have tried to love good people. I asked myself why I couldn't love them. Loving or not loving is fine. You only need to avoid acting against true feelings in your heart," Magnolia responded.

Our favorite waiter brought some Shakshuka with freshly baked bread to our table. Even if he asked each time, she was never going to give him her number.

"I don't know if it's you, the lake, or this food, but I will always come back to this place," the warrior said to the artist, and we smiled at each other. Differences can separate people, but they can connect them more strongly, too.

I spent the next four days with Freedom sitting on a blanket close to the lake, writing, reflecting, and resting.

I thought about Magnolia's words and reflected on my biggest love stories in my journal. *I have tried to love someone bad who didn't mind me being homeless, and I don't know why, but I don't regret it. I have tried to love someone good who loved me from the first dinner, but I don't know why I was able to forget him.*"

"You let it go because you used your power to simply accept it," Freedom said while bluntly staring at the lake in front of us.

"What about going against your feelings?" She looked at me and asked about the part of the conversation with Magnolia I'd been avoiding reflecting on.

"I'm not sure," I answered, and put my pen in the middle and slapped my journal shut with both hands.

Are you still in town? Daan texted me after I returned to the orange house and sat down on the terrace in the afternoon.

"You don't want to make Love mad in the beginning of your learning, right?" Freedom asked, more careful than usual.

I started typing on my phone.

"Hope isn't a feeling. It's just a thought. Don't follow it," she insisted.

"We will just hang out as two fellow travelers," I said.

She clicked her tongue and looked at the sky with annoyance in her eyes.

"Be careful not to break someone's heart while having fun," I heard her call from behind me as I walked downstairs to join Daan for a motorcycle ride. "I tried, Love, I tried," Freedom said to herself, frustrated and resigned. "And his taste for motorcycles is so bad." She sighed and sat on my chair to watch paragliders from the terrace.

Daan and I rode along the lake and through little villages nearby. Embracing someone funny and kind was comfortable and easy. I kept looking at the sky, which was changing from simple blue to a dreamy shade of pink as the sun slowly set. Daan stopped on the road close to the lake and took the first picture of us. Afterward, we ran toward the water, holding hands and laughing, almost like lovers.

"Your hands are cold. Let's head back for dinner," he said, embracing me in the warmth of his arm as we walked toward the motorcycle.

"Let's go," I said.

And he started to drive.

The whole way back, the motorcycle made clanking sounds as if it was about to break, but we both ignored it, pretending that everything was just right.

We arrived at the restaurant, which served my favorite pakora (spiced vegetable fritter) and his favorite wine.

"I would love to travel like you, do all the things I dream about," he said as his woodsy cologne distracted my mind. "But I recently moved into a beautiful house, my work is great, and making time to travel is hard. I wish I could be as strong and brave as you are," he continued.

I silently drank my wine. Every heart needs its own reason to change or speak up.

"Would you go with me to the Chitwan National Park to spend a few days in the jungle? We could get to know each other better," Daan asked when I finished my glass of wine.

Hope can be dangerous. Sometimes it attracts me to decisions that ignore reality and my feelings, creating an illusion that makes it difficult to find my way back toward my heart.

"I guess so. Yes, we could go," I answered and suddenly felt full of joy.

"The bill, please!" Daan paid and drove me back to my orange house.

Freedom usually waited up for me, but not this time. She enjoyed taking our small hard bed just for herself.

"We need to pack," I whispered to her, but she pretended to be asleep, so I packed everything by myself.

The next morning, she wasn't angry or disappointed but completely relaxed. "It's your life, your choice," she said peacefully when she saw the insecurity in my eyes. "At least I will finally see some tigers," she winked at me, and we walked outside.

It feels good not to be alone sometimes, I thought to myself and got into the car with Daan. The taxi ride was as long as our flight to Bharatpur, twenty important minutes, which were supposed to give us more time to get to know each other and maybe fall in love.

When we arrived at the charming resort close to the jungle, two Nepali girls put bracelets on our wrists and said, "We wish you to be happy here."

All the plants around the complex of rooms were perfectly cut, each door was locked with big decorative golden locks, and calming music was always played in the restaurant. The resort was separated from the world by a river and several hectares of grass, and trees where elephants and buffalos walked freely, sometimes enjoying and sometimes avoiding the sun. The path going through the middle of the resort was surrounded by little lamps strung between black poles. The lime and mandarin incense, which burned almost everywhere, gave the wilderness a spa-like feel, making people feel adventurous and relaxed at the same time.

Daan and I walked toward the river and stopped on the bridge leading toward the elephants' fields of grass. When thunder started to darken the sky, he kissed my dry lips. Cold raindrops slowly touched my head, face, and arms, then suddenly poured down my entire body.

"Run!" Daan shouted, grabbed my hand, and we followed the path illuminated by little lights toward our room. It felt like a movie in which the main actress didn't want to act.

The next morning, we went with a tour group on a safari trip to the Chitwan National Park. Freedom was still hoping to see tigers, but they were nowhere to be found. They left their footprints on our path last night.

"Well, sometimes, no matter how much we want something, footprints are all we can have," Freedom lamented in her sarcastic way.

Suddenly, the tour guide spotted a rhino. "Quiet," he whispered.

The entire group got to their knees to observe the animal from behind some tall grass. After a few moments of tension, the rhino disappeared, and we kept walking through the wild forest until we reached the river, where canoes were waiting to take us back. Daan was walking in front of me, and I watched as his brand-new hiking shoes left footprints in the mud.

As our canoes departed from the riverbank, he took my hand and said, "I know that we don't know each other well, but I'm ready to change my life and join your journey."

I'm sorry. I can't. was the answer I had rehearsed in my mind over and over again. But it wasn't true. I simply didn't want it. I didn't want Daan. That was the truth I needed to tell him. There was never a perfect moment to kill someone's hopes or break someone's heart. So I knew it had to be now.

"I don't feel it, even if I have tried to change the way I feel by giving us time," I said to him as we stood among the most beautiful and unexpected jungle scenery.

He cried. He tried to love again, only to fall apart once more because of my unwilling heart. My heart wasn't empty, though. *Not feeling something isn't the emptiness of one's heart. Those are the footprints left by true love. You can follow them to find it or ignore them to comfortably arrive at the closest destination, leaving love behind.*

Love was waiting and waving from the riverbank when we arrived right before the sunset.

"What did I miss?" Love asked Life.

"Her trying to make you real," Life responded and finally took off her glamorous hat.

"How could that be if I wasn't there?" Love asked.

"Well, she was trying but eventually decided to never again leave you behind," Life answered.

After the jungle adventure, we came back to the room and started to prepare our backpacks to leave Daan and Nepal.

India

MAY – JULY 2019

Follow the River

"What are we going to do here?!" Life looked at my bare, dirty feet as we stood together with Love, Freedom, and Death at the banks of the longest river in the Indian state of Kerala during the unpopular rainy season.

"We will study ancient natural medicine—Ayurveda," I said to her with a mysterious smile.

"What kind of idea is this?! Why?" she asked, terrified. Dirty feet didn't match her glamorous style.

"Because every great warrior must master the art of combat as well as the art of healing," I repeated my father's words from the time before he left my family behind.

"I see. But how are you going to earn a living? I know that your high heels are uncomfortable, but you invested *years* into your career, and it kept you secure," Life answered with a skeptical tone in her voice.

"Time spent doesn't measure if something is right for me. Security can't be someone's path, only the shelter in which you grow enough to fly," I answered.

Life looked at me with contemplating eyes for a moment.

"You're right," she said, finally taking her shoes off as well before playing in the mud with her feet. "I think that I know your—" Before she could finish her thought, Death interrupted her.

"Let's go and check out the area!" Death probably knew everything about life but still loved learning and studying more than any of us.

We walked through a landscape of giant palms, plumeria plants, and herbal gardens toward the facilities of the Ayurvedic school. I entered the first building where students studied the oldest medical system under learned doctors and practiced yoga. Then I went upstairs to the spacious top floor and looked around. There was a separate space for a yoga class and two classrooms. Between two doors to the classrooms, there was a big table with a golden candle stand, fresh white and pink plumeria flowers, and the pictures of Hindu gods: Dhanvantari (god of Ayurveda), Shiva (god of destruction), and his wife Parvati (goddess of fertility, love, and devotion). It was also the place where teachers and students together started each day with the chanting of the Dhanvantari mantra, bowing their heads, and fully devoting themselves to protecting health and destroying diseases.

I went back downstairs, walked outside, and passed the rooms of students and patients, doctors' offices, and treatment facilities. I headed toward the Ayurvedic restaurant where everybody ate and where they offered cooking classes every Tuesday. The restaurant was empty as it was still too early for dinner. There was only a girl sitting at one of the tables. She was dressed in a bright purple kurta (a loose collarless shirt) with a black bindi dot between her eyebrows. Her glowing skin and thick, long black hair made her look like a Bollywood princess. She couldn't be one though—she laughed with waitresses speaking their local Malayalam language with an air of more casualness than any royal life would ever allow.

"May I join you?" I asked her.

"Sure. My name is Niomi. You must be my classmate. The only one, as it seems."

"Karolina," I introduced myself and sat at her table. "You speak Malayalam, but you don't seem to live in India," I said, surprised.

"I was born in Switzerland, but I have my roots here," she answered.

"What brings you here?" I asked as she ordered turmeric milk and cookies for both of us.

"I'm taking a short break from my marketing career to learn something I always wanted to explore, just for a moment until I find my motivation again," she said and smiled at the waitress who set down her favorite golden milk and cookies in front of us. "What about you?" Niomi asked.

"I follow the steps of my mother, who is a healer, to see if my path is different or the same," I answered as I reached for a cookie.

"That's great. Trying is the best way to discover and become yourself," she said, and we both finished our golden milk.

A little while later, dinner was served. We ate as if the meal was our own little celebration. It was the last evening before both of us would try to change our lives. Trying already changed everything in us. It recognized that our hearts were more important than a lifeless resume and a king-size bed from which we woke up unhappy.

My alarm clock went off at five-thirty the next morning. Snoozing wasn't needed anymore; I no longer wanted to postpone feeling alive. I took a quick cold shower, put on loose white linen clothes, and ran barefoot to the spacious last floor of the next building which I had visited the day before. I sat on my yoga mat next to Niomi, whose eyes were still half-closed, and in front of the yoga master, who was sitting in a lotus position, looking very comfortable in his loose orange shirt and white pants. He was one of India's yoga champions, but he didn't speak much and made us follow him in silence. Even if it felt strange in the beginning, my body understood him better than my overflowing thoughts.

Niomi woke up in the middle of the class but still looked forward to the last posture, in which she could lie down on the floor without any movement for one moment longer.

After a couple of deep breaths, we sat together in a crossed-legged position and chanted 'om' with the master, whose vocal vibrations circulated around the hall and passed through our bodies before coming back to him. We closed our eyes and brought our hands together in front of the chest, connecting everything known and unknown as one.

Niomi opened her eyes first, looking energized and excited.

"I dreamed about this moment for such a long time. I can't believe that our Ayurveda classes start today." She looked at me with watery eyes, and I smiled. I loved watching new beginnings, not only mine.

Niomi changed her yoga clothes for a black and white kurta with elephants woven into it and put her glasses on. My simple black t-shirt was less fashionable, but I was lucky as studying bare-foot befitted us both.

After having a nourishing Ayurvedic breakfast and grabbing a thermos full of hot ginger water, we went upstairs again and joined the doctors for the chanting of the Dhanvantari mantra. We bowed our heads in front of the Hindu gods for the first of many times. A few minutes later, we walked into the classroom and sat on our wooden chairs with a small table attached.

The teacher wrote on the whiteboard: "Ayurveda—the science of life." We started to learn about the principles, doshas (three energetic forces that exist in every person's body), individualized nutrition, healthy lifestyle and daily routine, natural therapies such as oil and powder massages, sweating procedures, and other methods which use solely the power of nature to cure the human body. We devoted our days to learning how to perceive the health of ourselves and others as much more than the mere absence of diseases. According to Ayurveda, health is an active process of caring about the body in the way it needs and deserves and reconnecting it with nature—the only force which unconditionally gives us strength and keeps us whole.

After morning classes, Niomi was the first to head toward the restaurant. The staff loved her—waitresses told her their secret crushes, and the cook always invited her to the kitchen to try his traditional dishes of Kerala before he served them to others. She had that incredible energy of a person who is connected with her purpose and shines on her path.

After we ate, she ordered golden milk and cookies for both of us again, creating space to discuss everything we learned and how our perspectives were changing. I told her the story of my beast. I understood it better through everything we learned. It felt strange, but my heart didn't need to change my past.

"How do you feel about your deadly disease right now, after learning so much?" Niomi suddenly asked as if she could read my mind.

I considered a moment, then replied, "The beast taught me to love myself in the most difficult times, and now I'm stronger for it. I also understand and can help others who struggle with similar experiences. I could never wish to erase all of that."

Niomi looked at me with what looked like pride. Not letting go, but being able to see things from a positive perspective was the last step to closing my difficult past.

A strict and nerdy doctor started our afternoon classes. He liked to make his points while energetically gesticulating with a black marker in his hand. Each time I asked him a challenging question, he pushed his glasses up on his nose and took a moment before he answered. Niomi observed our intensive discussions without interrupting, peacefully sipping her warm ginger water.

One afternoon, when we had reached joint conclusions about seasonal dietary, the doctor switched to another topic.

"When Ayurvedic medicine fails to heal, yoga comes in and tries to cure the incurable," he said.

His words left me speechless. Yoga had been my powerful morning ritual that also helped me to heal my beast. I was sitting there alive, confirming everything that he went on to say next. Maybe it was more than a cure for my body and a ritual to start my day. Maybe I should have seen it as the beginning of something much bigger instead.

After the theoretical classes, we walked downstairs to start practical sessions, during which we learned how to do thera-peutic massages, conduct healing procedures based on ancient techniques, and prepare natural medications for different health conditions. Afterward, we washed our hands clean of medical oils, herbs, powders, and decoctions, then returned to the last floor for pranayama class with the same silent yoga master with whom we'd started our day. During that last hour, we practiced various tech-niques for controlling our breathing which helped us to finish our days with clear minds and oxygenated bodies. Such practice made us go through our transformation mindfully, accepting inevitable changes and loving them despite all the fears that can live even in the bravest hearts.

When the class was over, Niomi was always the first to stand up from the cross-legged sitting position, and I'd follow her toward the restaurant for dinner. Afterward, there was nothing better than falling asleep, feeling that even if nothing was clear in my life, I could still trust the process and feel joy.

After a month of the same routine, we understood the basics of Ayurveda and the cause of diseases. We mastered therapeutic massages and other procedures to strengthen the body from the outside. The second and last month of our course of study was devoted to learning how to strengthen the body from the inside. We learned the health properties of various plants, herbs, fruits, and vegetables, how to prepare a suitable herbal medication, and how to design a supportive diet for a particular person and his disease. Ayurveda differs from Western medicine in this way. It aims to heal not a disease but the whole person. Even for patients who shared the same health condition, we were taught to look for unique solutions tailored to the particular body constitution and the story of the individual patient sitting before us.

One afternoon after morning classes, Niomi and I sat drinking turmeric milk as always, although without cookies as we'd promised each other to stop eating them.

"I already know. I feel it!" Niomi said excitedly out of the blue, quickly setting her cup down on the table.

"What do you know?" I asked.

"I will give up my marketing career and continue Ayurvedic education in Switzerland to become a professional practitioner," she said.

"You understood your dharma—the purpose in life which serves you and others," I said with an admiring smile, repeating the things I'd learned in India. "I am proud of you, my friend," I added.

She rapidly took a sip of her milk to avoid having to answer, overcome with her emotions.

"What about you? How do you feel?" she asked after a moment.

"I don't feel as certain as you, not yet. I will keep looking and shaping myself with everything I learned on my way," I answered as Dhanvantari, the god of Ayurveda, watched us from the wall.

After weeks of waking up at five-thirty every morning for yoga class, Niomi had had enough. She wasn't a morning bird and needed a lot of sleep to make her shine. So I practiced with the silent master alone, opening and understanding my body more every day. It almost felt like silently falling in love, not with the beast anymore but with my healthy self. The master instinctively knew when I'd crossed another physical limitation or understood something meaningful through my practice. He still insisted on staying silent but observed me attentively and encouraged me to forgive my body for any imperfection and give it space and time to feel. I understood that not only healthy nutrition, herbs, and treatments keep us content and alive but also a conscious feeling of who and how we are right now—with our body and mind, emotions, life situation, and everything that has happened to us so far. In the end, we are not only living but also feeling beings, which makes us special but, at the same time, unable to live happily if we ignore our hearts. To me, yoga became not simply an exercise but a movement through which I was discovering with my body how to process and understand everything that was happening in my heart. To feel myself and be truly alive.

One day, the master finally spoke at the end of class, asking me to move my yoga mat and sit closer to him. "You're the future teacher. I suggest that you follow that path," he said shortly, breaking the silence after such a long time.

I brought my hands together in front of my chest and bowed my head. He did the same, then turned toward the table that held images of Hindu gods and prayed. It had to be him who decorated the table with fresh plumeria flowers every morning before everybody else woke up.

"Namaste," he said to me, then slowly stood up and left.

Life was standing close to the window in the same spacious hall watching the river flow by below. She turned around, walked toward me, taking up her yoga mat on the way and placing it next to mine, then sat down in a cross-legged position.

"You're so calm, neither excited nor surprised. It seems that you already knew about that path. Is that what you were trying to tell me at the river on our first day here when Death interrupted you?" I asked her.

"Maybe. But it was good that I didn't say it back then," Life answered, weaving her fingers together and stretching her arms behind her back.

"Why?" I asked.

"Would you consider taking such a different path from your previous one if I had said it instead of someone 'real'?" She smiled as if her plan was playing out perfectly.

"Probably not. A 'real' person bringing up your idea makes it seem more possible. Easier to try," I responded.

After two months of intensive study, we walked back to the riverbanks with our bags packed. Death, Love, and Freedom were already waiting for us there.

"Damn you, you always change everything," I said jokingly to the Periyar River. "Especially when I need it," I added and smiled at the river appreciatively.

"The world needs rivers as much as finding happiness needs effort and trying," Life added as she stood in the river, joyfully laughing and splashing water at me.

"Has anybody seen my shoes? I need to find them before we

leave. They are the most comfortable ones I have," Freedom asked, walking along the river, lost and confused.

"You don't need them. You were born without them, and you'll get along just fine now that they're gone," Life said, calming her down.

Indeed, we were all born, and can always decide to live, without them.

Periyar River, Aluva, India. May 2019.

Parvati

"I think that I'm losing my mind," I said to Freedom when reading a book about Hinduism during my connecting flight from Delhi to Dehradun in Uttarakhand, one of the Northern states in India.

The images of Hindu gods seemed to be moving, breathing, and changing. Lord Shiva looked at me with his unpredictable eyes set in his blue face. His hair was decorated with the crescent moon, symbolizing his timeless existence. The Ganges was peacefully flowing from his divine head. His handsome body was draped with tiger skin, which emphasized his fearless nature. Being one of the most important Hindu gods, along with Brahma the Creator and Vishnu the Preserver, Shiva held the role of Destroyer. It was he who removed the old and paved the way for the new.

Right next to him was Parvati, his wife, dressed in a beautiful red sari and adorned with fine anklets and bracelets. As the goddess of love, fertility, marriage, and devotion, she complemented Shiva with her motherly softness. In the Hindu stories, she reincarnated several times to marry him against her father's will, to save him when he drank a powerful poison, and to make him care about the world again when he abandoned his duties to mourn his previous wife. Without Shiva, there was no Parvati, and without Parvati, there was no Shiva. India wouldn't be the same without them both.

After my first months in India, I trusted gods and rivers more than ever before. I decided to follow the most sacred river, the Ganges, which flowed from the head of Shiva to Rishikesh. This town is known as the capital of yoga and meditation. It is located in the foothills of the Himalayas and on the banks of the Ganges. My yoga teacher training program had already started two days ago and was supposed to last for a month. I arrived at the reception desk drenched in sweat and completely exhausted after traveling from South to North.

"You must be Karolina," said a tall and much younger man with black hair tied in a bun on the top of his head. He passed me a glass of water.

I looked into his brown eyes for a moment without saying anything. I was exhausted. Or maybe distracted by the unusual brightness of his brown eyes.

"Yes, I'm Karolina," I answered before the silence became awkward.

"My name is Arjan. Everybody left to celebrate Lord Shiva at the Ganges but will come back after the sunset. You must be his missing and beautiful Parvati," he said with an admiring smile. "Let me show you the room where you will stay." He lifted my backpacks and walked through the empty hall toward the last room on the ground floor.

I rested on my bed before the group came back for dinner. Two hours later, I was awakened from my nap by the noise of twenty pairs of feet walking through the hall headed toward the dining area. I followed them to the tables. My fellow students came to Rishikesh from various countries and with different intentions—to transform themselves, others, or both. The same framework for learning could lead people, including myself, to many different life scenarios. I didn't necessarily need to know what scenario would come for me afterward.

Each time I tried a new path, I didn't expect to find clarity on what I should ultimately do. That wasn't the point of my journey. Rather, the goal was to discover myself in thousands of different ways. It was me, not the path, that I was looking for. Understanding that, I could take risks, learn, and succeed or fail with joy.

So there I was, simply discovering and connecting with another part of myself.

Teaching yoga has a divine history. It began when Lord Shiva taught his wife Parvati eighty-four postures of yoga. He didn't want to share it with anyone else except her. She, however, always cared about mankind and persuaded him to share his miraculous secret with people. Thousands of years later, we were sitting on yoga mats with our backs straight, trying to understand and experience yoga as something more than the wellness regimen and extensive flexibility presented in the pictures.

The morning bell rang all over the big hall at five AM sharp. Before I left for my journey, having a schedule felt like being locked in a prison. Yet during the last months, it felt like a framework for progress. The day started with a calm Hatha yoga class, which balanced the entire body and mind through postures and breathing. Afterward was a pranayama class during which I could continue expanding the capacity of my lungs and the ability to intentionally manage my breath. Breakfast was a great pause to center myself in the calmness and the way it made me feel—connected with my body and myself. The program continued with teaching methodology, including adjustment of postures, philosophy, and anatomy, which fascinated me the most as it made my self-discovery profound, tangible, and possible to comprehend.

During lunch, I always sat next to my philosophy teacher and let myself get lost in discussions of the essence of teaching. To become a teacher, it wasn't enough to equip the brain with all the knowledge available to learn. I had to nurture a heart like Parvati's that could lead with compassion—to give a piece of my being to anyone who was willing to learn from me.

After my body absorbed new energy from the food, it was time for an intensive and dynamic Ashtanga yoga class. After the first week of my new routine, I faced my first doubt. *I'm not strong enough. I'm not flexible enough. I can't follow the sequence of movements fast enough. How could I ever teach others?* I stopped following the class and rested in the Balasana pose, sitting on my heels, arms back alongside my thighs with the palms facing upwards and with my forehead on the yoga mat. Watery drops slowly slid down from my face toward the ground. It wasn't only my sweat. I cried like a child.

"All bodies are enough. Yoga teachers don't need to be gods. They need to teach that self-love is important, as if it was divine, and confirm it with their own heart," Freedom said after coming closer and gently patting my back with her hand.

"Freedom, you always consider all of us enough," I whispered into my yoga mat, exhausted.

"Trying despite your weaknesses and imperfections is what makes me proud," she said, and I accepted it while slowly closing my eyes.

Arjan found me as I was walking toward my room after the class. He touched my arm from behind with his dark-skinned hand and asked if everything was alright.

"I'm not sure," I said, looking at the ground.

"Parvati, sadness doesn't make your heart less divine." He didn't ask more, but it felt as if he was familiar with my darkness.

We walked to the garden together and sat on the grass.

"Then she was born as Meenakshi with beautiful green skin…" He understood that I didn't want to talk, so he started to tell me stories about the different incarnations of Parvati.

The stories calmed me like a child. They reassured me that I wasn't the only one going through transformations. Parvati transformed thousands of times—fearlessly, learning who she was all over again and never doubting herself. Her example was leading me from darkness back toward myself.

"Come on; you need a break. I will show you around." Arjan led me through the hall and outside toward his motorcycle, and we rode off, leaving a dust cloud behind us.

We followed the Ganges, passing never-ending hills, which made green my new favorite color. We stopped at Arjan's family house to have a meal of delicious Aloo Tamatar Jhol (steam potatoes with tomato and onion curry) served with pooris (fried puffed bread). The dish was made by his mother according to the recipe of his grandma, who was still working in the rice fields at the time we arrived. Everybody anticipated that incredibly tasty food and arrived at the table right before serving. Nobody was ever late for meals out of respect that bordered on worship for his short and quiet but powerful mother.

"Is *she* your Parvati?" his mother directly asked Arjan.

I blushed.

"We need to go now." He kissed her on the forehead without answering.

It was the time of Sawan Shivratri, the festival marking Shiva's wish to strengthen his union with Parvati. It wasn't a special time for me but for the traffic. Thousands of devotees of Shiva were heading to Rishikesh to worship him and seek his blessings. We slowly followed them on the motorcycle all the way back.

When we arrived almost three hours later, Love was waiting for me in front of the school entrance with her arms crossed.

"And?" she asked curiously, wanting to know how I felt about him.

"He isn't my Shiva," I answered and opened the school door to pass through while another teacher stopped Arjan on his way to talk.

"You know, Love. When people are focused on discovering their powerful true selves, they naturally turn away from stories or things that they don't want with their entire hearts," Freedom said, then cracked her neck and brushed the dirt from my lilac kurta.

After months of intensive studying, it was time to leave India.

"Parvati!" Arjan called after me as I was walking through the school door with my backpacks on and heading toward the airport. He put a bracelet made of green stones on my wrist. "She was born with beautiful green skin..." He repeated the words from one of his stories. "I was happy to witness you being reborn as someone so powerful." He kissed my forehead goodbye.

"Thank you, Shiva." I hugged Arjan one last time, looking over his shoulder at the portrait of the Destroyer, who dissolved my doubts and made me want to keep discovering myself with my entire heart.

Poland

AUGUST – SEPTEMBER 2019

The White Dress

I answered the phone and heard the Healer crying like never before, not being able to catch a breath to say anything.

"Mom, breathe with me. Calm down. What is happening?" I said to her in a controlled and slow voice.

"She can't... die," the Healer whispered, her voice shaking as badly as ever.

I looked at Death with scared eyes. "What have you done?"

"I'm sorry. It's time." Death took a deep breath and tried to stop the tears flowing from her pearl eyes.

"We went with Grandma to the hospital because of her headaches. She was diagnosed with terminal cancer. She doesn't have much time left. Maybe a few weeks," the Healer said, and for the first time, there was no hope in her voice.

"I talk to her every day. It can't be true. I would know. How—? Why—?" The pace of my voice fluctuated from urgently fast to desperately slow and barely audible.

My life stopped. The whole world stopped. I didn't know where I was, who I was, and who I could still be without her. I sat on the floor and helplessly hit the cold tiles with my fists. I grabbed the bottom of Death's plain white dress with long flared sleeves and pulled on it like a child.

"Don't go. Don't leave me. Don't take her. Don't," I begged her.

She kneeled next to me and placed her pale hand on my wet cheek. After a moment, she smiled through her sadness and disagreed like a caring but strict mother.

"Close your eyes and breathe with me," she said.

And I followed. Even if it felt worse than dying myself, I knew that I didn't have the right to argue with her.

The warmth of her hand calmed me down and showed me vivid memories of good times like an old movie.

I was sitting on Grandma's beige sofa bed with the pattern of little dark flowers on it, which she always kept covered with a thick material to make it last for the next generation. My feet still didn't touch the ground, but my nose already recognized the smell of each of Grandma's dishes, which she prepared from her heart. After eating, she played our favorite song from the audio cassette, and we sang loudly as if we could sing well. After some years, my little feet finally touched her old brown carpet while I was sitting on that ugly sofa bed. There was no other carpet in the world with more of my footprints on it than this one—thousands of small steps covered with bigger ones.

"You are tall enough now," Grandma said and opened her bottomless wardrobe to give me a white princess-like dress that she had bought for me many years before without an occasion in mind.

"Am I a princess now?" I asked her with an excited voice.

"The future queen." She looked at me with a spark in her eyes, brighter even than the glittering dress.

The dress wasn't the only one that waited for me. Grandma did too. She patiently waited for my adult feet to come back to her whenever they wandered abroad—working on projects, traveling alone on other continents, or failing to understand love while speaking foreign languages. No matter how big and exciting the world was, there was no better feeling than walking again on that old, familiar carpet.

Suddenly, Death took her hand away from my face. The movie stopped.

"Let's go," she said. I was surprised she wasn't going to leave without me.

I packed my backpack and rushed to the airport. It was the first time in my life I was scared to fly. My watch seemed to move slower than usual. The sound of my foot tapping on the airplane floor was louder than usual. Death's face was paler than usual. Flying must have scared her this time too.

"We are almost ready to land in Poland," Death said and buckled up my seatbelt.

"I'm not ready." I looked at her with smudged mascara under my eyes and gulped slowly.

She said nothing, took my hand, and led me through the airport toward a taxi. After almost two hours of driving in silence, we arrived at home. The Healer opened the door and hugged me as if I had just survived a plane crash.

"I love you," she said without waiting for an answer and served me her delicious tomato soup.

The visiting hours at the hospital were over, so we sat at the round pine table and chatted about everything except the things that soon were going to change forever. My watch was still moving slowly, and it seemed that our sleepless night was never going to end. But it did. We eventually fell asleep from exhaustion.

The Healer left for work early in the morning. A few hours

later, I woke up and just kept staring at the ceiling without blinking. I took a deep breath to stop my eyes from watering.

"Grandma can't see me crying," I repeated three times and then finally got up.

Handheld showerhead—dropped from my hands.

Comb—dropped from my hands.

Wallet—dropped from my hands.

Keys—dropped from my hands.

After bending down over and over to pick it all up, I was ready to go.

I was halfway out the door when I realized I had forgotten to put in my contact lenses. I went back to the bedroom and took a little container out of the plastic bag from my hand luggage. I opened it and smelled lemons, which made me wonder for a moment.

"No time, no time, no time!" I focused again and put the first contact lens on my left eye, which started to burn and cry. "What the hell is that?" I noticed that a little bottle of lemon essential oil was open and had spilled in the plastic bag. "It can't be. It can't be. It can't be!" I repeated to myself while flushing my entire face with water. I turned off the tap and opened my eyes. I couldn't see through my burned left eye. "How could I?" I cried, not because of the pain, but because I was going to see my grandma for what could be the last time, and I wasn't sure whether one eye was enough to memorize her forever. "Grandma can't see me crying," I said again, trying to pull myself together.

I closed my left eye and ran out of the apartment toward the hospital. I walked up to the oncology department on the ninth floor and entered my grandma's room. She looked at me with those eyes of hers—one green and one brown. Her face and her entire body were slimmer than ever before.

"What have you done to your eye? Go to the doctor! Immediately!" She gave me an order before saying hi.

I couldn't argue with her. I walked downstairs to the eye department on the fifth floor.

"There is a granddaughter of the patient from the ninth floor with a seriously injured eye," a tired nurse with dark circles under her eyes informed a young eye doctor.

Seniors were queuing in front of the doctor's office. They looked at me, disapproving of my crumpled lilac kurta and baggy yoga pants from India but unanimously agreed to let me in first.

"It's a very serious burn. You may not get your sight back. But we will try. I will prescribe a medication and hope that you and your grandmother will be fine," the doctor said after the examination.

"Thank you." I looked at her indifferently and stood up to walk back to the ninth floor.

"Wait, your grandma can't see you crying like that." Death stopped me and wiped my tears before we walked back into her room during lunchtime. It was important to us both not to worry her.

"Everything is going to be alright, Grandma. I'm fine. We're fine," I said softly when standing next to her bed. I took the spoon from her weak hand to feed her after she had spilled the broccoli soup over her white nightdress—the same one she used to wear at home.

Death stood next to us, dressed in her most beautiful embroidered white dress. She looked stunning, but her dress paled next to the stained nightgown I had loved for years.

"Her dress is prettier. You're right," Death admitted with full acceptance.

"Stop pretending to care and trying to be nice!" I said to Death, tired, angry, and sad.

"Stop it, child. She truly cares. She has always been a part of us." Grandma touched my hand as she defended Death from her warrior, who would fearlessly fight by her side, but who had never been taught how to give up.

Grandma and I. Jastrzębie-Zdrój, Poland. August 2019.

Unspoken Okay

"Can you see her like me?" I asked my grandma about Death, but she didn't remember what had happened just a moment ago.

Her eyes were becoming more and more absent. Tumors were spreading faster than expected, and the biggest ones appeared on her brain. I kissed her forehead. I loved her so much.

"May I speak with you for a moment?" the head of the oncology department asked me from the doorway to our room.

I silently nodded and followed him toward his office.

"I need to release your grandmother from the hospital. There is nothing more we can do for her." He kept turning his pen around between his thumb and index finger.

I watched the movement of his fingers for a moment and then looked at his face.

"It's okay. We will go home now," I said with a calm voice, trying to convince myself that I was strong enough to prepare her for dying.

The Healer picked up the Hummingbird from the airport after work, then came to the hospital and drove us all to Grandma's apartment. It was messy but not in a lazy way. She must have struggled in silence for a long time. Flashbacks came back to me at that realization. She didn't join us for a Christmas trip to the mountains. She invited my mother for lunch more often than usual. She didn't want me and my sister to stay longer than two hours when we visited her, even after being away for months. She decided to keep the pain to herself.

I was angry because, despite the geographical distance, we were best friends who talked about everything every day. I wasn't a princess anymore and didn't become a queen as she had hoped, but she loved me the same throughout my entire life. It was the only thing in the world that was never going to change.

I collected the clothes scattered all over her light leather sofa, which she had bought a few years ago. The old beige sofa with dark flowers never got to serve the next generation. Time was like the god Shiva, who held the responsibility of destruction in the world, always making things go. I sat on the sofa together with Grandma, we opened albums with old pictures, and played our favorite songs. The Healer was cooking her favorite dish—mashed potatoes and beef roulade in a simple sauce made from beef broth. The Hummingbird made her laugh about simple things and ate doughnuts with her from the sweetest shop in town. Death brought a big plate with plum dumplings, which Grandma had loved since her childhood. I stood up, took the plate from her shaking hands, and put it on the table.

"It's okay. Sit with us." I smiled at her and placed another teacup next to mine.

"Stand up, Grandma, stand up. I know that you still can." The Hummingbird believed in her, even if her body was becoming weaker every day.

"Please pull my head. Pull my head. Pull it now!" Grandma answered illogically, and the Hummingbird looked at her with tears in her eyes.

"We don't have to. It's fine. Let's sit and eat doughnuts now," the Hummingbird sat down next to her again.

Even if Grandma didn't want to eat anymore, she looked at her younger granddaughter with loving eyes and smiled. The Hummingbird didn't insist, only smiled back and turned on the TV to watch Grandma's favorite soap opera. She safeguarded her joy of life with her entire heart.

When Grandma fell asleep for a moment, the Hummingbird and I went to the kitchen to prepare chamomile tea and simply be with each other.

"Our trip to Thailand is coming next week. What should we do?" the Hummingbird asked as she poured hot water into the cups.

"I will stay. I'm sorry. I know that you were looking forward to traveling together after such a long time," I answered.

"This situation breaks me, Karolina. I don't know how to be stronger." She looked at me with helplessness in her blue eyes.

"Soon, you need to come back to work. You did so much. Take a break, fly to Thailand. We're here. It's fine," I said to her, knowing that growing strength was scary and required time.

She hugged me tightly, and I could feel that her heart was hurting unbearably. "I love you," she said.

"I love you so much," I replied, crying only with my good right eye.

She flew to Thailand three days later.

Life becomes scary when the only thing that matters is the inevitable passing of time. Days and nights were long as we cared for Grandma around the clock, without any rest, falling asleep in turns. At the same time, we didn't want it all to end, as that would mean she would be resting without us forever. My tired brain couldn't separate days from nights, but there was one night that I will always remember because it almost broke me.

"Karolina," my grandma said quietly in the middle of the night.

I could always hear her from the next room, and I immediately came, lifted her from her bed, and walked with her to the bathroom. When I closed the door after us, she placed her cheek on my chest and embraced me with her weak arms.

"I want to die, my child," she whispered.

I gently stroked her dark, thick hair, my fingers carefully passing over the tumors on her head. *Grandma can't see me crying,* I clearly instructed my shaking heart and kissed her temple without replying.

"Are you okay?" Death opened the bathroom door and rubbed her sleepy eyes.

"We're okay," I answered, and she helped me carry Grandma back to her bed.

I opened my eyes in the morning.

How could I have fallen asleep?! I jumped out of bed and ran to Grandma's room.

She wasn't there.

"It can't be. It can't be!" I shouted out loud, clutching my head in my shaking hands.

I ran into the living room. Grandma was sitting on her light leather sofa and drinking coffee from her favorite cup, the one decorated with pink flowers. I looked at her bare feet on the old dark-brown carpet and moved my sight from her white nightdress to her smiling face. She was so alive, peaceful, and happy. Despite the scary moments I knew were ahead of us, I hoped to always remember her in that blissful way.

I made myself ready for a visit to her primary care physician. This doctor had known Grandma for over twenty years and was supposed to help us with getting all the medication and equipment we needed at home after leaving the hospital. I arrived at her office, where not a single piece of furniture had changed since the communist era.

"May I see her latest examination results from the oncologist?" the doctor asked. Her professional tone kept me calm.

"Here they are." I passed her the file, not understanding why I still felt hopeful even though it was clear that my grandma was going to die.

"Fuck." Her tone drastically changed, and she quickly covered her mouth with her hand. "I'm sorry." She looked at me as if those two words could help my breaking and tired heart.

"It's okay."

"You can pick up everything you need from the pharmacy based on the prescription I gave you. You need to be aware that the current stage of cancer is serious and could possibly result in coma and internal bleeding. I'm afraid that she needs to stay at home though, as most of the hospices have long waiting lists for admission. In case of any emergency, you can call the ambulance or come to see me—you wouldn't have to wait in the queue. The next step will be radiotherapy to help with her pain. Contact the oncology clinic as soon as possible." Her tone was professional again, which made answering easier.

"I will. Thank you," I said quickly and walked past her old furniture toward the door. I wished that I could burn it all. Nothing was meant to last forever.

I got back into my car, fastened my seatbelt, and started the engine. Then an immense feeling of powerlessness and hopelessness paralyzed my entire body. I wasn't okay. I was mad. I started to hit the steering wheel with my palms. I hated doctors for not being able to help. I hated myself for not noticing any of her signs. I hated time for passing too quickly. I hated Love, Life, and

Freedom for not being there. I hated Death for taking someone I loved, someone who I wanted to live so badly. I hated living after I had almost died.

"I hate it. I hate it. I hate it all! Forgive me, Grandma. For the first time, I'm giving up in the most important moment of our lives." I screamed so loudly that people who were passing by stopped and looked at me with scared eyes until I put my head on the steering wheel and calmed down.

I looked at my watch with my right eye and realized that I was late for my grandma's next dose of medication. Missing it could further shorten her fading life.

"No, no, no! No time for crying!" I wiped my face, breathed deeply, and drove back to Grandma's apartment. "Mom, medication!" I entered the apartment and headed toward the kitchen, where the Healer was cooking lunch.

"No worries, darling. I already gave it to her. I also arranged the radiotherapy sessions with the oncology clinic. They will start tomorrow," the Healer said with a calm voice.

"I'm sorry that I didn't stick to the schedule," I said.

She gave me a glass of water.

"We're here together. Remember?" She wiped tears from my cheeks with her healing hands. "Strength isn't about the lack of tears but the will to come back and continue your fight." She stopped stirring the soup on the stovetop and hugged me.

The next morning, my grandma, the Healer, and I walked across the old brown carpet together for the last time. I felt it. We passed through the door, and I carried my grandma three floors downstairs. These were the same stairs that she had helped me climb in my childhood. My mom opened the car, fastened Grandma's seatbelt in the back, and gently removed some stray hair from her forehead. She was safe. She was loved. She was still with us.

At the oncology clinic, the massive machines, radiation mask, and flashes of light didn't scare her. She was ready to die right after coming out of the machine and seeing my last smile.

The ambulance drove her to another hospital, where she was supposed to stay for two weeks during the radiotherapy. The Healer and I drove after them to make sure that Grandma was okay.

The Healer walked into Grandma's room, patted her pillow, and fixed the sheet under her mattress even if it wasn't needed.

"We will be back tomorrow with all your favorite things from home. I love you." The Healer gently kissed Grandma goodbye on her forehead as if her mother was a little girl again.

"I can't believe that soon we will see her for the last time," the Healer said before opening the car door.

"I'm grateful for having the chance to say I love you and good-bye," I answered.

And she started to drive.

When we reached home, the Healer's eyes were red and swollen.

"Are you tired? What's wrong with your eyes?" I asked.

"No," she answered and walked toward the mirror.

"Did you cry?" I asked.

"No," she answered, then looked in the mirror and recognized that her eyes were red from infection. "It's a virus. I can't risk infecting her. Today was probably the last time..." The Healer stopped blinking while staring at her bloodshot eyes, and tears slowly ran down her cheeks. It took all her strength to stand still, control her breath, and keep her heart from falling apart right then and there. 'I love you.' She was going to remember those three words as her final goodbye. "I can't leave her. I can't leave you like that." The Healer cried the whole night.

"It's okay. We aren't going to be alone. Death is with us," I said.

Death nudged me, and I bit my tongue. She didn't want people to know she was always around.

The next day I cleaned, cooked, and asked the Healer to rest. She was powerful but still human. I started to drive back to the hospital, and after two hours of driving, I realized that I could see the road with both eyes again. I gently touched my left eyelid with my left index finger.

"Are you okay?" Death asked from the backseat when I arrived at the hospital parking lot.

"Don't you see what is happening? How could we be okay right now?" I answered in an angry voice, then got out of the car, and loudly slammed the door.

Death stopped me before walking into the hospital and said:

"It is okay to hide a difficult truth if you do it not because of fear but out of love.

It is okay to escape from what breaks you when you know that you will come back stronger.

It is okay to be a coward for a moment when you need to be heroic all the time.

It is okay for your stressed body to give up when somebody you love needs you.

It is okay. But right now, you need to be calm."

Warm Feet

One, two, three, four, five, six pairs of feet, all different shapes and sizes, were resting on metal beds in the rooms I passed by in the hospice ward. All of the different long or short stories of their lives converged here, to this place where they were learning the same hard lesson of accepting the inevitable—eternally cold feet.

The walls separating their rooms were full of pictures of smiling patients who understood that simple joy overcomes the biggest fears, even the fear of dying. Freedom walked slower behind me and studied the pictures one by one, her eyes full of compassion and fascination. Even if she was walking silently, her glowing dark skin and flowy orange dress made it impossible not to draw attention to herself, and eyes followed her from every bed.

When I reached the middle of the hallway, there was a kitchen corner with a fridge and a table with chairs where people could sit and drink tea or coffee. Nobody in the world cared more about enjoying the best taste of coffee than in that place. There were two male patients sitting in their wheelchairs, drinking cups of espresso, sipping it slowly with looks of immense joy on their faces. After I passed them, I turned left and saw my favorite feet in the world—uncovered, toes impatiently moving, as if trying to reach the edge of the mattress to stand up and go.

"I'm here, Grandma. I'm here." I grabbed her big toe in the same way she used to when I didn't cover my feet with a duvet during my childhood.

She looked at me with angry eyes, threw her water bottle at me, and shouted as loud as she could, "Get me out of here! I don't want to be here. I want to go home!"

I stood dumbfounded and stared at the water bottle on the floor. I picked it up and put it back on the table. "It's okay, Grandma. I love you," I said calmly and unpacked her bags.

I placed her favorite slippers right next to her bed, even if she was never going to walk again. "Home is where your feet stay warm," she used to say when I stopped believing in an evil red duck with horns. It was our home. Our last home.

"I need to do your pedicure again. Tomorrow is your birthday. You can't lay here with feet like those," I said to my grandma, believing that living was still more important than dying.

"Can't we do it tomorrow?" she asked with a scowl on her face.

"You taught me never to postpone things. You can't change it now," I answered.

And she rolled her eyes.

"Visiting hours are over," said the nurse, who never smiled back at me as she entered the room right after I finished Grandma's pedicure.

"We're ready now, Grandma. You can go to sleep," I said and covered her feet with the white sheet and warm blanket. "Goodnight."

One, two, three, four, five. One pair of feet was missing from the first room when I came back to the hospice the next morning. I was walking slowly through the hallway with a birthday cheesecake for my grandma in one hand and two little cups of espresso for the gentlemen sitting in the kitchen corner in the other hand. I placed the espressos and two pieces of cake on their table on my way.

"Good morning! Today is my grandma's birthday," I announced with a happy voice, and they asked me to sit down with them.

"What's your name?" the bald man sitting on my right side asked. He had a ship tattoo on his arm.

"I'm Karolina," I answered.

"I'm Jan, and this is Adam," he said, and they both tried the cake without asking for more details about my life. I was sharing my joy. It was enough.

"This must be heaven!" Adam, who was much younger than me, said even before trying his espresso, which I'd gotten from the best café nearby. He ate another spoonful and offered me a bite as well.

"You're right. Heaven!" I said with the voice of a happy child.

"You're always welcome to join us at our table whenever you have time," Jan offered with a wide smile.

"Thank you! I have to go to my birthday girl now, but I will see you tomorrow." I looked at them both and felt excited. It was probably the only place in the world where simple celebrations were worth more than gold.

One, two, three, four. Two pairs of feet were missing in the room next to my grandma's. I walked a few steps more. *Her feet are still here,* I thought to myself when I peeked through the door to my grandma's room.

"Happy birthday to you," I started singing while walking toward her bed. Her eyes were half-closed and her mouth slightly open. "Grandma?" I came closer and gently shook her arm, trying to control my growing panic.

"She received a strong medication to help her sleep better at night and still hasn't woken up," the daughter of a neighboring patient said, trying to calm me down.

"I will help you with serving the cake," Death interrupted as though wanting to distract me.

I put a tiny piece of cheesecake to Grandma's lips, and she moved them slightly.

"I love you." I kissed her forehead with my trembling lips.

She opened her eyes with difficulty and answered quietly, "I love you, too." Shortly after, she fully closed her eyes.

"Grandma?" I asked again, but she breathed heavily and stayed quiet.

"Love gives freedom when you learn how to accept me," Death interrupted the heartbreaking silence and straightened the overwhelming amount of Grandma's falling dark hair on her pillow.

I walked to the end of Grandma's bed, grabbed her big toe, and touched her feet. "I promise to keep my feet warm until I'm at your side again."

"Go now. She doesn't want you to drive back home at night," Death said.

I drove back to our hometown to take care of the Healer, doing what Grandma would usually ask me to do.

Six, five, four, three, two, and one. The car engine stopped, and I arrived.

Always and Forever

When the Healer opened the door, I looked at her with both eyes.

"You can see! You can see with your left eye!" She was so happy she almost cried.

"Yes, I'm fine. I'm fine, Mom." I touched her arm to calm her down.

Her blue eyes were bright and almost clear of the redness. She was healing herself faster than ever before.

"Karolina, she..." Death tried to say something as we were walking to the kitchen.

"I can smell your tomato soup!" I said to the Healer, interrupting Death.

"Karolina!" Death insisted.

The Healer had started to serve my favorite tomato soup when her mobile phone rang. "I don't know this number but let me see who's calling." After a minute, she looked at my feet on the ground and hung up. "It was her last birthday. She died." Her legs started to shake, and she couldn't take a breath.

"Sit down. Sit down, Mom. Give me your hand," I said to her and led her toward the sofa. "It's okay. It's okay. It's okay."

I hugged her and stroked her short blonde hair as she started to cry.

"I wanted to tell you... It was her time." Death sat next to me on the sofa and rubbed my back.

"I already knew." I turned my head toward Death, and she quickly wiped her tears. She didn't want anyone to see her crying. "Thank you for caring and being with us all this time." I held the Healer's hand, and Death held mine.

The Hummingbird came back from Thailand to the United Kingdom, where she lived and worked. After a few days of catching up with her responsibilities, she caught another flight back home to take care of us. When she arrived at night with three white roses, we didn't cry. We were going to stay strong together, as my grandma always wanted.

The next day, the massive wooden door of the church creaked open, and people dressed in black walked in to fill the pews. The Hummingbird, the Healer, and I walked behind them, carrying white roses and holding hands. Love, Life, Death, and Freedom followed us, wearing matching black suits and black mourning veils. When the priest came to the altar, we all stood. "Amen." No more of his words could go through my empty mind.

After the mass was over, the Healer walked forward and opened the massive wooden door again. The priest headed toward the cemetery, and the people all followed him. When we arrived at the columbarium, the priest asked me whether I wanted to pray again before locking her ashes in the marble wall forever.

"I will always love you." I took the urn into my hands and placed it in the columbarium, sure that love was the most powerful prayer we had ever had.

A week after the funeral, Grandma's apartment was almost empty. I opened the bottomless wardrobe and said goodbye to the white dress she had given me when I was a little girl. The Hummingbird was organizing Grandma's clothes to donate. The Healer was watering and packing her beloved plants. Freedom was cleaning the apartment. Love was sorting and packing our photographs. Life was organizing all the utility bills and ownership papers. I was sitting on the old brown carpet and looking at the family picture frames standing on the shelf above the TV. She had looked at them every day for years.

"I'm so sorry, I couldn't…" Death started as she sat next to me on the carpet, but I put my finger to her lips.

"Stop it. I know. You didn't have a choice. It's okay," I answered.

And she hugged me like a friend who had almost lost me.

"It's so strange. She is gone, and one day I will die as well, but it still feels like I'm going to love her forever," I whispered to Death, hoping that nobody else could hear me.

"You don't need forever. Love doesn't exist to make your heart eternal but limitless," she whispered back and, with a look of deep reverence and surprise for the pristine condition, touched the old brown carpet, which had somehow resisted the passage of time.

Kyrgyzstan

OCTOBER 2019

Never

Stop, let go, and change—those three tasks pushed other priorities out of my life. Stop crying. Let go of the pain. Change direction to find new ways of looking for strength. I started with the last one. My previous plan was to fly to Japan to continue studying natural medicine and energy healing techniques. But I couldn't focus on learning how to heal others when I needed to heal myself.

"We aren't going to Japan as planned," I said to Love, Life, Death, and Freedom a few days before our flight to Tokyo. I canceled the reservation on my phone.

"Why?" Freedom asked.

"I need a change. I can't live in the old ways," I said.

"What about going to the mountains?" Freedom knew where I could find my peace.

"They are also in Japan," Life added. She always considered things in the most practical way.

"But I need new heights, ones that have never come across my mind before, to find clarity and become stronger than ever," I said and opened Google Maps on my phone. "Never before, never before..." I mumbled to myself and turned the Earth around with my finger.

"Are you really going to choose the next country so randomly?" Life asked, surprised.

"What do I have to lose? I have already lost so much," I said without taking my eyes off the map. "Kyrgyzstan in Central Asia—surrounded by mountains, unexpected, and different enough," I said with sudden confidence in my eyes.

"What?!" Love, Life, and Death reacted in the same surprised way. Freedom clapped her hands.

Soon we boarded a plane to Bishkek, the capital city of a country which I'd given the thankless role of lifting the heaviest heart.

"What do we know about Kyrgyzstan?" Love asked from the window seat, wearing her gray sweatpants and an extra-large hoodie. For the first time in a while, she was exhausted and didn't care how she looked.

"Over centuries, it was invaded by Mongolia and the Russian Empire, among others. It later became a part of the Soviet Union." Death seemed to recall the entire history of Kyrgyzstan directly from memory as if she had seen it play out with her own eyes.

"It finally gained its independence when the Soviet Union fell apart at the beginning of the nineties," Freedom added in a peaceful voice with a wink at me as if she had a secret part in it.

"Smart girls! But what are we going to do there?" Life asked impatiently.

"Look at the mountains! They're stunning!" Love pointed at the giant mountain range through the window. "How could you ever be bored this close to the roof of the world?" Love grabbed Life's shoulders with unexpected excitement.

"It's beautiful, but I need to rest." I looked at Love with my sad, blue eyes. My heart was so tired. Pain was constantly boiling inside it, and I felt almost as though my heart chambers would burst from the pressure.

"We all need to rest sometimes," Life said with compassion as we got off the plane.

We picked up our backpacks and walked through the airport, looking around with curiosity.

"Taxi! Taxi!" I tried to stop one of the old cars coming and going on the road in front of the airport entrance.

The old man wearing a red flannel checkered shirt and a brown beret from the eighties stopped his car, got out, and helped me put my backpack into the trunk.

"Where to?" the driver asked.

"We should go directly to Osh Bazaar and eat. I'm terribly hungry!" Life suggested.

"To Osh Bazaar, please," I answered.

I was grateful for Life's suggestion, as I didn't know where to go. I felt indifferent about the entire world. I didn't care about the possibilities, the adventure, and I didn't want anything more that life had to offer. My heart had stagnated.

We got out of the taxi and walked through the bazaar gates into the crowd. The bazaar was lively, loud, and colorful—a serious contradiction to how I felt internally. There were countless stalls full of fresh vegetables, fruits, herbs, homemade bread, marmalade, honey, cheeses, pickled cabbage, and eggs from nearby villages. Endless passages led to further parts where everything else could be found, including tobacco, household goods, musical instruments, clothes, and jewelry. Hundreds of eyes wandered back and forth, hoping to find their piece of joy. Hands carried bags packed with more than people needed. Feet, mostly in old leather shoes, impatiently stepped from side to side, waiting to pay, trying to shuffle through the crowd, or trying to leave the bazaar through the gates. And there was me—walking around in my hiking shoes with empty hands and eyes cast down to the ground.

Life finally found the corner where smiling ladies wearing floral head scarves were selling warm homemade food—Manti dumplings, Ashlan-fu (spicy cold noodle soup with vinegar and chili), and Shashlik (grilled meat on a skewer). She made me try it all until my stomach was full.

"Eat more. Soon you will need to grow enough strength to allow yourself to give up," Life said, which made me furious.

Despite her good intentions, I couldn't hear anything through the clamor of feelings overwhelming my heart.

"What are you talking about?! You spent so much time teaching me how to become strong. Now you're feeding me like a baby and asking me to learn how to give up?!" I aggressively shouted at Life in the middle of the crowd.

Love, Freedom, and Death stopped eating their food and stood speechless next to us.

"I know that you're hurt, but trust me that soon you will understand," Life answered calmly and patiently as she looked into my teary eyes.

"I don't need you! I don't care! Just leave me alone!" I shouted and walked away.

Life grabbed my shoulder from behind. "Hey! Wait!" she exclaimed.

I turned around, and she hugged me unexpectedly.

"It's okay, my girl, it's okay. Everything is going to be alright," she whispered and gently kissed my temple.

I cried into her chest like a child, feeling for the first time in my life that I wasn't strong enough to rebuild my own heart.

"Let's take her to the Issyk-Kul Lake. She needs a break," Freedom said and took the bags of food from me.

"It's a beautiful lake, I promise." Life looked at me in the most forgiving way and grabbed my hand without hesitation. We walked toward the bazaar exit together. No matter how miserable I was and how much I hated being alive, Life was never going to give up on me.

Osh Bazaar, Bishkek, Kyrgyzstan. October 2019.

Proof of Life

I don't understand any of it, I thought to myself when trying to read the name of the settlement written in Cyrillic on the road sign. The driver stopped the old marshrutka (shared taxi van) and lazily announced that we had arrived in Barskoon. One long street lined with a few houses with old wooden picket fences and old classic Lada cars parked in random places—it was a spot simple enough to make me feel comfortable, stop wandering, and take time to face everything that was happening in my heart.

After a short walk, I stood in front of a blue guesthouse and knocked on the door. A woman opened it and smiled at me with her plump lips, puffy rosy cheeks, and almond-shaped brown eyes.

"My name is Begimai. Welcome home," she said warmly.

And I followed her through the yard to my room.

"I'm Karolina. Thank you for having me here," I answered as we walked into my small room. It was furnished with just a bed and one shelf, yet I was surprised at how easily my struggling heart accepted a strange and almost empty place as home.

"Have some rest and come for dinner at six in the evening. Please don't be late," Begimai said.

Before she left, she placed three caramel candies on my bed.

She closed the door and walked back through the yard where three of her little boys were playing. I watched them through a window for a moment before one of them noticed me and stuck his tongue out. I did the same. The boys giggled. It was a favorite greeting for all of us.

I closed the curtains and lay down on my bed. My body felt heavy and cold. Each muscle pressed me down toward the earth, and I started to shake. Something was trying to break through and leave my body. Pain? Sadness? Maybe my soul.

"Am I dying?" I asked Death.

"No. Feeling something is proof of life," she answered and rubbed my hands between hers to warm them up.

A little while later, still wearing her dirty kitchen apron, Begimai shouted through the yard, "Dinner is ready!"

I shot up and walked to the dining room.

"Albin, Omar, Zamir." She pointed at each of her sons, who were already impatiently sitting at the table and waiting for food.

"Hi." They smiled politely in front of their mom.

Behind her back, I stuck my tongue out at them again.

The incredible smell from the kitchen distracted us all. Begimai served Oromo (savory pie filled with cabbage, carrots, onions, and meat) and black tea.

"You all must eat everything to be strong," she said while looking at the boys. "Without exceptions," she added, looking at me, and then invited everyone to dig in.

I heard Love, Life, Death, and Freedom shoving each other in the kitchen and moving pots. It was clear to everybody that Begimai cooked from her heart, and eating her meals was pure joy.

"I like it here. This place gives me a family feeling." I overheard Life talking in the kitchen.

"It was a great idea for her to take some time and process the struggle. Thank you, Freedom," Love said.

"I think that we all need that time to stop and process things," Death said with a sigh.

"Of course, you can't go far if you're dragged down by a heavy heart," Freedom said, distracted by the lovely smells of the kitchen. She lifted a kitchen towel and uncovered a freshly baked apple pie.

"Woah! It smells delicious!" Life clasped her hands with excitement.

"Well done, everyone. Time for dessert!" Begimai stood up from her chair, and her footsteps disappeared into the kitchen.

She came back with slices of her pie on little plates, and everybody at the table watched her every movement as she served it to us. The first spoonful of juicy apples and crust, the second spoonful, the third—heaven! The pain paused for a moment.

"We have the first good sign," Life said to the rest after watching me from behind the kitchen wall.

"Just give her some time," Love added and waved at the others to head to bed.

"Goodnight," Death said to me and closed the kitchen door behind them.

The boys slid down from the chairs onto their little feet and politely said, "Spokoynoy nochi."

"Goodnight, Albin, Omar, and Zamir," I answered.

Begimai smiled. She probably didn't expect me to memorize their names so fast.

I helped her clean the dishes, and soon after, it was lights out. I covered my face with a thick blanket and fell asleep with my hands resting on my warm stomach.

I woke up with a frozen nose; I had uncovered half of my face to breathe during the night. I slowly moved my body toward the edge of the bed, threw off my blanket in one rapid motion, and ran to the warm shower, grabbing a towel on my way.

"Good morning! It isn't that cold. Why do you need so many warm clothes?" Freedom, who wore only a t-shirt, laughed at me while brushing her glowing afro in the bathroom mirror.

"Very funny!" I answered as I walked past her to grab my backpack from the room.

"Where are you going?" she asked, following me to the door.

"To the lake. Maybe it can teach me how to find beauty in my stagnation," I answered and closed the door behind me.

"Darling, breakfast!" Begimai shouted from the window and came outside to give me a packed sandwich for the road. In her eyes, there was no life when one's stomach was empty.

After following one straight road through the village and crossing the empty highway, I reached the Issyk-Kul Lake. Its stillness held so much space for my shouting heart. The roaring noise rose, spread over the calm blue lake surface, and reached the Northern Tien Shan mountains rising from the horizon. Losing someone hurt, I accepted that. The pain spread, and I allowed it to. Any future next to my favorite feet dissolved. I had to come back to the present, keep trying to stand up again, and walk through my future without her.

I came back home to Begimai with a smile on my face. I didn't want to worry anyone or spread my sadness. Stealing happy moments from others didn't seem fair. When I walked through the yard, the boys stuck their tongues out. Omar kicked the ball toward me as an invitation to join their game. I wasn't much of a football player, but they insisted on making me one.

At five o'clock sharp, the game was over. The boys went upstairs to their room, while I went to the kitchen to help Begimai with preparing dinner.

"This is the recipe from my grandma for the best Manti dumplings in the world." She showed me a page of her old hand-written cookbook, its pages covered in stains.

"I never thought to write my grandma's recipes down." I looked at her cookbook, and as my eyes danced across the scrawled handwriting, I suddenly regretted not doing so.

"You know, they won't live forever," she said while taking flour, salt, and eggs from the shelf.

"I know. Maybe those written recipes could make them live for a few moments longer," I said and started to cry.

I covered my mouth with a shaking hand, and Begimai quickly turned around.

"Did I say something wrong?" She hugged me and affection-ately stroked the back of my head.

"No, I'm sorry. I shouldn't cry," I answered.

"I understand. You loved her cooking, but she isn't with us anymore. I'm so sorry." She looked at the ceiling, trying to stop her own tears.

"I don't want to be weak," I wiped my tears.

"You aren't weak but visible." She looked confidently into my eyes while keeping her hands on my shoulders. "It takes a lot of courage to stop hiding your heart."

"Thank you, Begimai." I embraced her a bit tighter.

"Now, let's prepare our Manti dumplings." She released me from her arms, closed her cookbook, and passed me a big red bowl.

After dinner that night, I went to bed, hugged my knees to my chest, and cried for many hours. My body was shivering, and the pain changed into strange sensations, like electricity crawl-ing through my veins. A fever was gradually spreading from my head toward my feet, creating layers of sweat on its way. "Are we...

giving up?" I asked my body in a scared voice. As soon as I'd asked that question, I calmed down. I understood the answer.

Strength wasn't only defined by how stubborn I could be to keep going forward and fight, but also by whether I could become brave enough to give up and accept it as proof that my heart was still alive.

After I fell asleep, Life covered me with a blanket. "Tomorrow, you will stand up for the first time in a while," she whispered, then gently kissed my forehead goodnight.

The Warrior Queen

When I was a child, I asked my grandmother whether I was a princess. She told me that I was much more—destined to become the future queen. Even if I was far from true royalty, I still believed that making efforts to grow my heart was enough to make her proud. I couldn't disappoint her now. I had to grow my heart strong enough to stand up and keep going for her.

After two weeks, the boys didn't stick their tongues out anymore but hugged me tight with their little arms.

"I will miss you, Albin, Omar, Zamir," I said, hoping that they would remember me as the passionate football player they trained me to become.

Begimai prepared one last breakfast sandwich for me to take on the road. "Be well. I wish you lots of courage—to go forward but also to stop. Whatever feels right," she said and kissed my forehead.

It was time to leave for the mountains, which always offered clarity for my struggling heart.

"Why do all marshrutkas have to be so loud?" Life complained after we'd all piled into another old van on the main road.

"Stop complaining about things you can't change," Freedom answered her, taking a seat close to the window.

"I'm grateful for these great drivers. Imagine if we had to get behind the steering wheel ourselves." Love sat next to Freedom and looked at the gear shift, which worked only after multiple attempts by the driver to change gears.

"If Life was a driver, I'm not sure if we would survive." Death laughed from the seat behind us.

"If any one of you were driving, I would definitely get out," Freedom said and opened her tiny packet of kurut—dried salty yogurt balls, a traditional Kyrgyz snack.

"Karakol!" the driver said loudly after almost two hours.

We got out near the eastern tip of Issyk-Kul Lake, a great starting point for our hike. Most of the surrounding mountains weren't accessible during that time of the year. The choice was easy—follow the sun and be faster than the snow.

"Al-tyn Ara-shan," I read out loud slowly from the map posted on the wall of the hostel after we checked in.

"It's a lush green gorge up in the mountains with curative hot springs," Freedom said and sat on a chair to clean her hiking shoes with a brush. "It's also home to rare snow leopards, which were trapped by hunters and sold to zoos all over the world during the Soviet times. Now they enjoy nature in peace, staying invisible to people," she continued, and her dark brown eyes brightened as if directly reflecting the sun.

"The kingdom of snow leopards." It sounded almost too surreal to be true. I started to prepare my backpack. "You took care of my shoes, too. Thank you!" I kissed Freedom on the cheek, and she smiled a bit uncomfortably. She never learned how to be affectionate, even after hanging out with Love for so long.

"Always," she answered and walked toward a tent that served as a bedroom in the big hall of the hostel.

"Did you come up with the idea to stay here?" Life asked

Freedom that night as we lay next to each other, packed like sardines.

"No. It was our girl being too strict with her money," Freedom whispered, hoping that I wouldn't hear.

"Goodnight, ladies." I closed my eyes and fell asleep with dry cheeks for the first time in a while.

The next day, Love, Life, Death, Freedom, and I hiked five hours through autumnal scenery to reach Altyn Arashan and its breathtaking mountain landscape, hot springs, dense spruce forest, and the Palatka Glacier looming over the river. We walked toward the guest house, entered our room, and sat on the hard beds, completely exhausted. We only had enough energy to jump into the hot springs, eat, walk back to the room, and fall asleep.

The next morning, the host introduced me to Esel, a man in his mid-twenties who wore a red chunky-knit hat and the kindest smile I had ever seen. He took care of our host's two horses, Messi and Orlik.

"Nice to meet you, Karolina. Come and meet the horses," Esel said after introducing himself.

I followed him to the road where the horses were patiently waiting for him. I stood in front of them unmoving and watched them with a nervous smile. The moment I touched Orlik's brown shoulder, he peacefully squinted his eyes, and all the memories came flooding back.

"Did you pack everything for your horseback riding summer camp?" Grandma asked as I was tying my shoes in the hallway of her apartment.

"Yes!" I answered excitedly and then ran downstairs.

My father was there to pick me up and drive me to a horse farm outside our town. As our family became a mere break from work in his schedule, I often didn't feel loved enough. The horses could feel that. They loved me double to compensate for it, and I loved them back with my entire heart. From the time I was six years old, I trained in horseback riding every other weekend and every summer at camp. Growing into a warrior became more peaceful and easier through my passion for horses. When I rode, I was above everything that hurt me and away from things that I couldn't change. I couldn't imagine having grown up without them.

"One day, you will have your own horse, I promise," Grandma kept repeating to me, knowing that nothing else mattered to me more than my family and riding horseback.

After seven years of riding horses, one day the Healer asked me to come to the kitchen and sit at the round pine table. She'd just received the doctor's opinion about a condition I had in my spine.

"I have difficult news." She sat down next to me and took my hand. "You can't continue riding horses. I'm so sorry."

"But Mom—" I tried to say something, but I couldn't. The pain in my young, passionate heart silenced all words.

"I know." She cried with me. "But everything is going to be alright." She stood up from her chair, came closer, and hugged me. "It will be alright. It will be alright," she repeated a few more times, like a spell that might heal my back.

"Have you ever ridden a horse?" Esel asked, bringing me back to the present.

"I have. For many years," I answered quickly and looked down.

"Do you want to ride?" he asked.

"It has been a while. I can't," I answered, trying to silence my heart.

"Of course, you can." He put Orlik's reins into my hand and mounted Messi.

I quickly put my left foot in the stirrup and swung my right leg over the saddle. As I did, the feeling of powerlessness left my body through my feet and disappeared into the ground. There was no way to change my past. I had to embrace it through acceptance to claim it as a powerful part of my life. The part that didn't continue in the future but made me a person I was there and now. An excitement rose from my feet through my entire body, flowing toward the sky. I could feel joy again.

"Where are we going?" I asked Esel as the two of us rode, me slightly behind him.

"Lake Ala-Kul up in the mountains," he turned around and answered. "I knew that you could do it. You never forget how to ride!" he shouted enthusiastically as we rode through green meadows toward the Arashan River.

After we crossed it, the horses patiently stepped higher and higher until the clouds covered the mountains. The green meadows changed into stones, the blue sky turned gray, and the cold wind froze my pale hands.

Esel suddenly stopped Messi and pointed at the top of the rocky mountain. "We will see the lake from there."

I got off Orlik and looked straight up at the giant mountain. Its fantastic height dwarfed me. "It's impossible to climb up there!" I said to Esel, and he started to laugh.

"You can do it. I know you can." He started to climb up, leaving the horses behind.

I shook my head from side to side and started climbing the rocks with my frozen hands, following Esel's confident steps.

Right before I wanted to give up and simply roll off the mountain, Esel took one last, long step, turned back, and said, "Give me your hand! We made it!" He helped me up, and there we were, both standing at the top.

Esel stood behind me, put his hands on my shoulders, and slowly walked us forward toward the mountain edge.

"Our most beautiful lake is there." He pointed through the fog and clouds, but I couldn't see anything.

After a few seconds of silence, we both started to laugh at the same time. Even after our long climb, I didn't feel disappointed. The only thing I wanted was to laugh. I missed it so much. That feeling was more important than what my eyes missed now.

"For a moment, I was afraid that she wasn't going to make it all the way up," Love said, concerned, and hid her nose in her big, green woolen scarf.

"She is always stronger than she thinks," Life answered, looking at me with pride.

"She is stronger than ever before as she learned how to accept the things she can't change," Death added.

"Like losing someone she loves or something she can't live without?" Freedom followed Death's thought.

"She is so much more than everything that she has lost and is going to lose." Death took a deep breath and led us down the mountain, carefully removing each unstable rock on our path.

When we finished descending, Messi and Orlik were still waiting for us in the same place.

I gently touched Orlik's white forehead with my index finger. "Hello, my love," I said to him with a peaceful heart.

Everything I had lost didn't carve a dark hole inside me, leaving me incomplete but rather made space for me to continue discovering myself. Nothing was lost. Nothing could hurt.

We got on the horses, and before we headed back, I looked up at the thick clouds in the sky.

"Grandma, I don't need my own horse anymore," I said to her with full acceptance. "Even if it was impossible, I became the Warrior Queen when standing on my own feet."

Suddenly, the first snowflake, followed by millions of others, drifted slowly from the sky. I knew then that she'd heard.

"Hurry up, Karolina! We need to make it back soon," Esel shouted and started to gallop through the hills.

"Are you ready?" Love asked while embracing me from behind on the back of the horse.

I held the reins tighter and made the *cluck-cluck* sound with my tongue, pressing my legs on Orlik's sides.

"Here comes the Warrior Queen, who was born from a thousand tears and claimed her power among millions of snowflakes," Life said, watching me fearlessly gallop through the giant snowy mountains. It was more than that sad little girl could ever envision she would discover and conquer, when her small world was falling apart.

Before climbing up to see the Ala-Kul Lake.
Terskey Alatau mountain range, Kyrgyzstan. October 2019.

The Philippines

NOVEMBER 2019

Sometimes

"Dear guests, welcome to El Nido! Even if we would like you to enjoy our paradise, a typhoon is around the corner. We need to keep you safe," the hostel manager announced in a nervous voice right after I arrived on Palawan Island; the place where I had come to continue my search for joy, close to the sea, white sand, and swaying palms.

The wooden banca boats didn't take anyone to the beautiful lagoons, a destination on many travelers' bucket lists. The moored ferries didn't allow any new dreamers to arrive and forced those who were already there to slow down and live their dream differently. El Nido was calm and silent—qualities most people usually couldn't find either there or in themselves. Without any rush, queues, and crowds, peace of mind became the only thing for all of us to explore. I wasn't any different from the others trapped on the island; I was learning how to be happy without being constantly distracted from what I truly felt.

"Even a postcard paradise needs to rest sometimes," Life said, then walked out of the hostel, looked at the cloudy sky, and closed her long, yellow raincoat.

"Sometimes things aren't as scary as they seem. Let's see that empty beach." Death walked out after Life without any fear of the upcoming thunderstorm.

Love giggled, left her umbrella in the hostel room, and followed Death. Freedom shrugged her shoulders, grabbed her black leather jacket hanging on the side of her bed, and walked out as well. I looked at my raincoat but decided to leave without it. We were fine with the rain.

"We aren't made from sugar," I said, repeating one of my grandma's favorite sayings as I closed the door behind me.

By the time we reached the beach, the rain had stopped. There were seven little Filipino boys playing rugby with two American tourists. They played using a coconut as the ball.

"You are in!" One of the men threw the old coconut toward me.

I caught it in my clumsy hands, and the little players started to run after me. After making a few circles on the beach, I gave up and fell in the sand. The four fastest little players tried to take the coconut out of my hands, but I didn't want to make it too easy for them. The other three boys ran toward the tall and muscular American player with glasses, who gave them a final high five for their overall great performance. I looked at the impatient boys close to me and knew that I had kept them waiting for far too long.

"Let it go right now," Life said, tickling me on the sides of my body.

"Let it go." I exhaled and felt joyful.

The tallest boy grabbed the coconut from my hands and ran back toward his American coach, triumphantly finishing the game.

The American coach came to me and introduced himself, "I'm Bradley."

We sat on the sand, watching the storm clouds cover the

rocky hills, as they slowly disappeared on the turquoise sea horizon.

"Karolina," I replied but didn't tell him anything else about myself and my life.

"It's strange. We can't do much here, but I don't feel like leaving," he said, still panting heavily after the game.

"Why is it strange?" I asked.

"I can't remember the last time I stopped to enjoy simple things and focus on breathing," he answered and took a deep breath to slow down his heartbeat.

"Sometimes I wonder why people can't understand that their hearts weren't made for endless running," Love said when throwing up her hands.

"Resting scares them because it makes their hearts softer," Freedom responded.

"Softer means easier to hurt?" Life asked.

"No. Easier to heal," Freedom answered just as the rain was about to start again.

"Why would they be scared of healing?" Death asked, raising her bushy eyebrows.

"Because it requires them to learn what hearts sometimes consider impossible—to fall in love with Life again, despite her being the cause of their biggest scars," Love answered and prodded Bradley to protect me with his jacket against the pouring rain.

El Nido, The Philippines. November 2019.

The Suitable One

"Stop! Stop right now!" Life shrieked at the typhoon after a few days of persistent rain. She liked slowing down but couldn't stand it for too long. Nature never resisted her, and the first rays of sunshine broke through the clouds not long after she'd commanded it.

"Calm down, Life. The typhoon is almost gone. Our plane will depart soon." Love patted her on the shoulder.

"Where are we going now?" Life asked, surprised. She still hoped to sunbathe on a boat in beautiful lagoons.

"Siargao Island," Freedom answered, as the next destination was her idea.

She knew from the beginning that a few days of enjoying one of the most popular paradise destinations would be enough, as we both didn't like to be anywhere crowded for too long. She chose a teardrop-shaped island with thousands of palms as the best place to restore my power in a new way—not riding horses but riding waves.

"Surfing! I can't wait!" Love said with excitement, after we boarded the plane. Then she tied her ginger curls into a ponytail and put on her golden aviator sunglasses.

We landed, and not long after, were sitting on the beach right next to our hostel in General Luna.

"Why are you crying? Look around! There are palms, turquoise waters, dreamy beaches," Love said when she saw two tears running down my cheeks.

"Because I feel joyful, and I shouldn't. It's too early." I couldn't help but feel guilty for trying to be happy so soon after my grandma died.

"Joy doesn't deny your pain but gives you permission to stop feeling broken for a moment." Love took off her sunglasses and looked into my watery eyes. "Only in those soft moments can the deepest cracks on your heart start to seal," she continued while combing my hair with her fingers.

"I'm going for a swim." I stood up, ran to the sea, and dived into the waves.

After floating back to shore, my warm and salty feet walked toward Love again. I stood in front of her, about to say something, when I realized that while her ginger curls were the same, her eyes were somehow different—not hazel but blue.

"Oh gosh, I'm so sorry. I confused you with someone," I said to the oddly familiar woman standing on the beach close to the hostel.

"No worries. I'm April," my fellow guest introduced herself with a British accent.

It was remarkable how alike she looked to Love with her delicate features, charming freckles, and long, messy ginger curls. We stood together chatting on the beach for a bit longer, and for the first time in a while, I felt that I wanted to reconnect with people. April laughed easily and joyfully, even if her life story wasn't a bed of roses. Her stunning beauty was attracting many wildly handsome men, who were teaching her how to choose better instead of giving her a real chance to love. Despite all of her dangerous romantic choices, she never gave up on opening her heart again. After listening to her stories, I was full of admiration for her patience. She already understood what she was worthy of and knew that finding it was just a matter of time.

"Are you girls ready for a trip on mopeds?" Sergio, who worked at the hostel, approached us and wasn't able to take his eyes off April. He was Irish, much younger than her, and didn't fit into the sequence of her previous choices—he was too short, too chubby, too kind, and too funny.

"I don't understand why people are distracted by so many details. I'm not short or tall, skinny or full-figured, funny or serious, ginger, blonde or brown. My only important trait is being suitable or not." Love's irritated voice interrupted the story unfolding in front of me.

"Here is your helmet, honey. Sit behind me," Sergio confidently said to April, who blushed in response.

She turned around, blinked at me playfully while shrugging her shoulders, and Sergio started to drive.

Six other hostel guests and I followed them on mopeds down the palm tree-lined road leading out of town. After every kilometer, April embraced Sergio tighter and tighter, which made me smile at the birth of something wonderful and miraculous, this time in a way that was so simple and quiet. After two hours of riding, the whole group stopped for a break and walked to a secluded paradise beach.

"What are you doing here?!" I asked Love, who was unexpectedly sitting alone on the white sand, wearing her aviator sunglasses and drinking a fresh coconut through a bamboo straw.

"Did you say something, darling?" April asked me.

I paused for a moment and looked at the turquoise sea. "He

is so different from the men in all your stories..." I said while looking at Sergio, who had gone for a swim.

"I used to choose the same wrong type of man and believe that
I could change the inevitable unhappy ending. Now I know that
the right choice creates my happy ending from the very beginning,"
April said as her big blue eyes magically changed from amused to
a look of falling in love. "What kind of man would you choose
for your partner?" April asked as we looked at the men around us.

"One who brings me joy," I answered and gazed out at the sea.

"Is bringing joy enough to make someone a suitable partner?"
She took a tube of sunscreen out from my backpack and smeared
some across her shoulders.

"It's the only thing my heart needs for sure right now," I said,
smiling on one side as I put more sunscreen on my legs.

"Well, maybe it's a good start. Better than entirely giving up
on opening your heart," she said. Sergio returned from the sea and
kissed her cheek.

"Come here for a moment," Love called to me from her spot
on the beach, away from everyone.

I walked toward her. She asked me to sit down next to her,
took both of my hands, turned them upwards, and gently touched
the lines on my palms with her index finger.

She read the story my heart was destined for:

"Broken heart wants to rest.
Rested heart wants to find joy.
Joyful heart wants to feel.
Feeling heart wants to love.
Loving heart wants to grow."

"Let's move to the next step and find joy," I said confidently.
I trusted her process without hesitation.

Food for the Heart

Freedom opened the curtains in the early morning right before my alarm clock went off. Siargao wasn't for sleeping—it was a surfing paradise, where everybody woke up together with the sun. Throw on a bikini, smear some sunscreen on your face, grab a bite of banana bread on your way out the door, and pick up your surfboard—there were four precise steps before running into the sea every morning.

Freedom always brought along her beautifully crafted wooden surfboard and patiently taught others how to embrace the feeling of being powerful and humble at the same time. The waves didn't accept anyone who tried to ride them without learning her lessons. Those who understood them started their days with deep gratitude for the moments of unity they found with the wildest element that could heal and teach but never be tamed.

Wet bikini, salty hair, dirty feet, and tired smiles marked the time for breakfast. A Filipino woman dressed in a long white linen dress brought delicious yellow mangoes cut in cubes to the table and shared them with everyone. She mixed mangoes with organic granola and almond milk in a little bowl made from coconut and started to hum a song I didn't know.

Suddenly she stopped, looked at me, and introduced herself with a male voice, "My name is Iris."

She looked almost mystical. Her brown skin was glowing, defined dark curls made her look wildly desirable, and her masculine hands were strong and angelic at the same time.

"You must be an artist," I said to her.

She nodded in confirmation.

"She is a pretty good singer," Sergio added while bringing a cup of coffee for April.

She was indeed a good singer, and her concerts in General Luna became one of our regular evening outings. Her voice told the story of a thirsty heart, which was visible even when covered by the long, dark curls with sunshine highlights that rested on her chest. Whenever she sang a romantic song, her brown eyes always went back to the same hostel guest in the crowd—Jonathan. He was tall, always walked barefoot, his long hair smelled like coconut, and his shy smile made him mysterious and attractive at the same time. Sometimes his eyes seemed to love Iris back, but he controlled himself perfectly, staying faithful to his usual romantic standards.

After one of her concerts was over, Jonathan grabbed my hand as we were walking out of the bar.

"Is it me or her who should be holding his hand?" I asked Love while Iris was packing up her guitar on stage to join our group for dinner.

"Neither, my dear," Love answered with a slight irritation in her voice and started to walk toward her moped.

"Why are you so irritated?" Freedom asked Love, walking next to her.

"Because she is distracted, and somebody else is coming," Love answered as she dug through the pockets of her shorts, looking for the keys to her moped.

"It's alright. She isn't getting married tonight." Freedom rolled her eyes and yawned while getting on her own bike.

Love, Life, Death, and Freedom drove back to the hostel and fell asleep without waiting for me to come back.

Jonathan and I walked through the streets and in and out of bars holding hands. It was the first time in a long time that I was a simple girl foolishly laughing, drinking wine, and kissing someone without trying to memorize the shape of his lips, the things he liked, and his plans for the future. We walked a long way back to the hostel at the end of the night, and he hugged me before going back to his room.

"Goodnight. I had so much fun." He kissed me on my cheek.

"Me too. Goodnight." I kissed the tanned skin on his arm.

After releasing me from his embrace, I walked toward my room, where I lay down, still smiling.

"How was it?" Freedom whispered while I was sneaking into my bed.

"How is it possible that something so trivial made my heart stop aching for a moment?" I asked without answering her.

"In the end, hearts are human, darling. When they are hurt, simple feelings of joy are like nourishment that helps with healing," Freedom answered and made me hungry for another piece of banana bread before surfing in the morning.

The One Who Brings Joy

After catching a wave and enjoying that feeling of complete freedom for the first time in a while, I jumped from the surfboard triumphantly and stepped onto the reef, which cut a middle line on my sole. The streams of blood floated up from my foot onto the surface of the water. It should have hurt, but it didn't. It couldn't. The ocean became the place where I discovered my most powerful healing—to surrender and trust that my heart and I were going to be fine.

Sunny days, bamboo hammocks hanging between palms, and colorful sunsets made everyone feel dreamy. Sergio held April's hand under the table. Love was easy. Iris laughed when Jonathan broke the string of her guitar. Laughter was easy. Drinking bubble milk tea after eating kinilaw (raw seafood) didn't feel weird anymore. Joy was easy. The idyllic paradise made people forgetful, forgiving, and open to newness. In the evenings, hostel guests gathered in the kitchen space to grab a drink at a long wooden table with a beige macramé hanging on the wall above it.

The biggest questions were asked at that table:

"Who were you before?

Who are you now?

Who do you want to become?"

Answering those questions was equally important in everyone's paradise story. For so many people, traveling wasn't only about seeing places, taking pictures, and going on adventures. It was about going a distance to be understood—by themselves and others—away from everything that stopped them from feeling and being who they truly were. Travelers couldn't escape from the latter when telling their stories all over again. They also had to express themselves through thousands of everyday choices—destinations, things they liked to do, people they chose to hang out with, when they decided was the right time to stay or go. Bit by bit, they were uncovering their own shape, not relying on the world around them to sculpt their identity. Knowing who they wanted to become didn't require a reliable plan and impressive achievements. Discovering every day what they loved about the world and themselves was enough to eventually understand what they should do, where they should live, and why they were here.

"Mojito or beer?" Jonathan asked Iris in the kitchen at the hostel.

"Mojito." She made a quick decision and looked at him with loving eyes.

"I told you that it wasn't the best idea. Now it's kind of awkward here," Love whispered to Freedom while looking at the pair from her seat at the long wooden table.

"Love, it's fine. Relax," I said and poured more martini into her glass.

"Never mind. Here comes the sun," Love took a sip without offering any kind of explanation.

Life spotted the silhouette of a tall man walking through the hostel gate. "I'd know those black-and-red tattoos anywhere!"

As he walked closer toward me, the light from the kitchen revealed his perfect white smile, shoulder-length blonde hair, the guitarist's fingers, and the silver signet ring.

"Matching those two is a bad idea." Life looked at him and me, and then she turned toward Love, "How could you bring him here?!"

"Why not?" Love responded with a playful smile.

"She is not ready!" Life continued. "He isn't either."

"They will be more than fine," Love said confidently, right before finishing her martini.

"Hi, Max!" Iris greeted him in the kitchen space and gave him a cold beer.

"Who is he?" I asked Sergio, who was sitting next to me at the table.

"Another singer. He moved out from the hostel a day before you arrived but still hangs out with us sometimes," he answered.

"Apparently, somebody wanted to spare me that handsome trouble." I looked at Life.

I could feel Max looking at me from a distance when I stood up and walked toward the water dispenser to fill my bottle.

"Hi. I'm Max." I heard his voice sooner than expected.

"Hi. Karolina," I answered shortly, then turned around in an attempt to avoid trouble. I walked toward the beach, which was illuminated by little lights hanging between palms.

I sat on the sand, which was still warm from the sun, and watched the stars in silence. I was surprised at how easily I could enjoy romantic moments alone. After some time, I heard someone's steps approaching me from behind.

"Hi again." Max sat next to me, having escaped from the kitchen party.

"Hi again, stranger. Who are you?" I asked a usual question without looking at him.

"I'm a musician and DJ, a surfer sometimes. And you?" He sat next to me on the sand and looked at the stars as well.

"Lawyer, writer, healer, yoga teacher, and now surfer some-times," I answered while playing with my feet in the sand.

"How do you find time to do all that?" He looked at me, sur-prised.

"I'm still figuring it out." I looked at him and tucked my hair behind my left ear. "Is there something you're still trying to figure out?" I asked.

"How to be better at music all the time," he said and glanced at my lips. "I also love learning yoga." He smiled, and before I real-ized it, I had sunk into his arms.

"Aren't artists human, always enough as they are?" I said and dropped my cheek on his chest.

"Sometimes," he answered.

"Right now..." I said quietly and smiled.

It was getting late. I closed my eyes for a moment and sud-denly opened them, scared to lose control over my heart. I quickly kissed him on his cheek, stood up, and went to bed.

"So, that's it?" Freedom asked Love in surprise.

Love said nothing, shrugged her shoulders, and suspiciously giggled.

The next day, I had just come back to the hostel after surfing in the late morning when I heard someone singing in the outdoor common area. I walked in and followed the sound of someone's voice and guitar.

"I sang that part too high again." Max interrupted his singing with a self-punishing voice.

"I don't think so. I enjoyed it." I came closer, and he smiled.

"I have tried to perfect it, but it doesn't work. It makes me crazy." He sounded restless.

"Music is art. You don't hear it. You feel it. Why do you try so hard to make it perfect?" I asked, surprised.

"Because I want to be good enough," he answered. I just hoped that one day he would fully acknowledge his incredible talent.

"How could it ever last if he hasn't yet learned how to love himself?" Life asked Love skeptically.

Love sighed and looked at him with caring eyes. "He is almost there."

"Be realistic. Almost is not enough. When I almost did, almost loved, almost won—nothing ever happened or changed. Maybe they both should wait," Life responded, frowning her forehead and waving her hands in the air.

"I see your point, but let her decide," Love said in a calm voice, not sure what to do herself.

"Could you help me pick up my clothes from the laundry service?" I asked Max, following Life's usual pragmatic approach.

"Sure. Let's go," he answered immediately.

We got onto his moped. I hugged his waist from behind and looked at him in the side view mirror. I stopped myself from smiling. There was nothing more dangerous than falling in love with someone for who he was going to become in the future—the person who loved himself enough to share love with others.

After fifteen minutes of driving, Max stopped at the little ice cream shop on the way. "Come with me."

We entered the shop, walked out with homemade coconut ice cream, and sat at the wobbly table next to the road.

"What happens when a musician meets a writer?" he asked flirtatiously after starting to eat his ice cream.

"She keeps the memory of him in the book instead of her heart," I answered cheekily, and we both laughed.

"Let's pick up your laundry." He stood up and touched my warm, sun-kissed arm with his cold signet ring.

I picked up two bags of my clothes from the laundry shop

across the street while Max waited for me outside. Afterward, we headed back toward the hostel, when suddenly, he turned down a side street that wasn't along our route.

"I want to show you where I stay since you love yoga as well." He parked his moped in front of a beautiful yoga resort and asked me to come in.

Various paths surrounded by lush green palms, hibiscus plants blooming with red flowers, and neatly cut grass led to the vegan restaurant, a little farming area, wooden guest villas, and a space for practicing yoga. He grabbed my hand and led me toward his spacious boho room. He went to the bathroom to change his clothes. I looked around, quietly stepping on his wooden floor. I tried to comb my messy, salty hair with my fingers in front of the mirror, then quickly turned around when he opened the bathroom door.

"Pretty lady, I'm taking you out," Max said playfully, smelling nice and looking fresh in his loose white shirt.

I looked at my bikini and stained jeans shorts. "Great. Pretty lady is ready!"

My dirty and hurting feet walked over the neatly cut grass.

"Where are we going?" I asked as I followed him toward the moped loaded with my two laundry bags.

"It's a surprise." He waited until I was holding onto him to start the moped, then started to drive.

A few moments later, we arrived at the bar, where I could hear Iris singing from outside. We walked in, and April, who was there with our hostel group, greeted me with a kiss on the cheek and laughed.

"Gosh, doing laundry takes a very long time," she said.

Jonathan waved at me with a cold smile as Iris performed her favorite song. Max brought me a drink, and we both sat down.

"Max!" Iris called to him from the stage. "It's your turn." She started to clap her angelic hands.

Max jumped on stage, grabbed a guitar, and greeted all the musicians as well as the crowd. He started to sing the first cover song and his powerful voice circled the small bar, pulling people away from their phones and conversations. As he continued, people started to join him in singing. After a few more songs, it was clear that he was the undeniable king of his music. After finishing his gig, he sat behind me and surrounded me with his legs.

"My laundry is dirty again." I looked at my bags and laughed.

"We will do something about it tomorrow."

Max took a sip of his beer, and we listened to the next musicians together until it was late.

"Ready?" he asked.

"To sleep?" I turned around, still in his embrace.

"No. To love," he said and laughed.

"Sometimes. Not really. I'm not," I said, trying to answer the question for myself as well.

"Sometimes..." he repeated slowly. Without hesitation, he touched my lips with his index finger and kissed me.

Oh gosh! I thought in panic and out of joy. "Time to go home," I said instead before giving him another kiss and standing up. "April, should we go home?" I asked her, not seeing Sergio around anymore.

"Sure, darling, let's go," she said and waved goodbye to our hostel group. "How was it?" April asked after parking her moped in front of the hostel.

"It was good. Too good," I answered as we walked toward the dorm room. "Is there such a thing as enjoying something too much?" I asked from my bed.

"Of course not, silly girl. Joy always feels overwhelming for a healing heart. Goodnight," April answered and switched off the lights.

"Who is he, Karolina?" Love asked me while I was trying to fall asleep with my confused heart.

"He is the one I need to heal, the one who brings joy."

"Why are you so scared?" she asked.

"Because he made me feel again," I said quietly in the dark.

"Are you falling in love?" Love kept asking.

"No," I answered.

"To feel what then?" She tried to further understand.

"To feel happy even without her." Tears of relief ran down my cheeks as I knew that my grandma always wanted me to live this way.

"A joyful heart wants to feel. You made it, my girl," Love said, sitting on the side of my bed and crying happily with me for the first time. Even if there had been many misunderstandings between us, joy had brought us closer than ever before.

Siargao Island, The Philippines. November 2019.

Mexico

DECEMBER 2019

The Happy Land of Death

"¡Qué rico!" Death cried in joy, savoring her quesadilla with Oaxaca cheese and guacamole.

We were sitting at a little corner restaurant located in Oaxaca city across the square from where musicians were playing lively mariachi music. I ate another slice of seafood tlayuda (large, flat, crispy tortilla smeared with refried black beans, covered with string cheese, and topped with seafood) and raised my glass of red wine to make a toast.

"To Mexico!" Love, Life, Death, and Freedom clinked their glasses with mine, and I asked the waiter for another top-up.

We came to Mexico to learn about the highest form of joy that Life could think of—celebration. Mexicans could teach the world about lots of things, but nobody had them beat when it came to enjoying the simplest things with one's entire heart.

Life opened the map of Oaxaca city on the table and started to mark all restaurants she wanted us to visit.

"It's a lot! Can we eat in moderation, please?" I asked, trying to bring her back down to earth. But in Mexico, nobody wanted to live in moderation. Here, they enjoyed life to its fullest.

"Come on, let it go. ¡No pasa nada!" Life answered and smiled at the waiter as he refilled her glass with red wine.

"What happened to her? She is more relaxed than usual," Freedom whispered to Death.

"Last night, she told me out of nowhere that she didn't want to waste time on not being happy, and that I had all eternity to understand it." Death shrugged her shoulders and grabbed another crispy nacho with cheese, jalapeno peppers, and refried beans. "Spicy!" she said, and her face turned red.

Freedom poured water into her glass.

"¡Gracias!" Death thanked Freedom and placed her own cold hands on her cheeks.

After five days of exploring local restaurants and trying to grow accustomed to the impossibly pleasant level of spiciness, I started to pack at the hostel again. I missed the Pacific Ocean, whose waves always called me home. Life marked one of the best Mexican surfing spots on the map—Puerto Escondido. Since the moment I first stood up on the surfboard, Life and I knew that our home didn't need walls anymore; no walls could accommodate our infinite ocean.

"Ready to go?" Love asked and opened the hostel door.

"Ready!" I answered, lifted my backpack, and walked out.

"¡Vamos a la playa!" She impressed me with her Spanish, even if she spoke with her sweet Eastern European accent. The idea of living close to the beach made us all smile widely.

"Puerto Escondido!" the sweaty bus driver announced, after a few hours of driving along the bumpy roads, listening to sentimental songs from his entire lifetime. We got out.

It's already December. It had been almost three months since Grandma passed away, I thought to myself while looking at swaying palms, coconut stands, and old pickup trucks passing by with surfboards loaded in their beds. Time was flying fast. Maybe Life was right. Being happy was the only way to make sure that I wouldn't waste it.

"Not that I'm hungry again, but there are the best smoked fish tacos nearby. We haven't tried those yet," Death suggested gently. Her appetite for joy was increasing. She was usually quiet and calm, but that was changing as well. She stopped caring about what people expected of her.

"You know what? Let's get those tacos right now." I looked into her pearl eyes and took her hand.

She smiled in surprise, and we all ran to the little restaurant by the ocean. She was right. Those smoked fish tacos were incredible, so much that we all lost track of time eating them.

"Let's go and check into the hostel before it gets dark," Life said, wrapping her last taco in a napkin to-go and hiding a little piece of lime in the pocket of her comfortable baggy shorts. Her Hollywood look was gone for good.

We walked back to the main road and flagged down a taxi. A driver with a big, bushy mustache stopped with a screech of his tires. There weren't enough seats for five of us, so Death sat on Life's lap. She was the slimmest, even with her large appetite. After the fast and furious ride, the driver got out of the car and politely opened the door for us.

"Gracias..." Death said and looked at him with shocked eyes as she stepped out.

The hostel reception was still open. I handed my passport to a Mexican man with long, brown hair tied into a ponytail, who was drinking yerba mate from his calabash gourd.

"Hello, Imox. My name is Chac," he said when he saw my birthdate.

"Imo... What?" I asked, surprised.

"The spirit of water," he answered and showed me an ancient Maya astrological symbol on his phone. The heritage of indigenous civilizations is forever present in Mexico—not only in ancient pre-Hispanic stories but in the blood of descendants who continue cultivating their old knowledge through modern times.

Chac helped me with my backpack, and we walked together toward my room.

"Goodnight, Kemee," he bowed his head toward Death. He seemed to sense her and knew her Maya astrological sign as well.

"How do they know each other?" I asked Life.

"He knows Death through his ancestors. They taught him to celebrate her just as they celebrate me because leaving this world is as miraculous as coming into it," she answered, and a shy smile appeared on Death's face. "Chac also knows how much she loves food here. Every November, they both celebrate together with his ancestors, and she always enjoys trying their favorite meals," Life continued.

"On the Day of the Dead..." I added.

"Exactly," Death said in a cheerful voice. She kissed me on the forehead and wished me sweet dreams. Then she covered my feet with a blanket, the same way my grandma did during my childhood.

I fell asleep with a peaceful smile on my face in a land where even Death was happy.

Burn to Die

"Don't eat too much before the afternoon," Death told me as soon as I woke up the next day.

"Are we fasting?" I looked at her in disbelief.

"No, but Chac will take you for temazcal," she answered.

"What? Mezcal?!" I couldn't believe that her appetite for joy had grown so much that she wanted us to drink alcohol during the day.

"Te-ma-zcal," she repeated slowly and laughed. "It's the ancient Maya steam bath ritual—the moment of your rebirth," she added mysteriously.

Death walked toward Life's bed and pulled the blanket off her saying, "Enough sleeping. Time to get up!"

"Could you please be a bit more human sometimes?" Life rubbed her eyes and yawned.

A few hours later, Chac parked his pickup truck in front of the hostel, and we all jumped into the bed, taking seats on the piles of firewood he kept in the back. We drove to a remote piece of land with an igloo-shaped hut and fireplace in the middle of it. I looked up at the hummingbirds which flew from one surrounding tree to another, turning the sky above us into a spiral.

Chac unloaded the wood at the fireplace and put a colorful belt on his hips, symbolically separating his emotions and perceptions from the ceremony he was about to lead. The eagle man, as he called him, arrived soon after us and placed the volcanic rocks in the middle of the fireplace. Chac lit the fire, which he called the grandfather (abuelito fuego), and the heavy volcanic rocks woke up from their profound sleep, becoming the grandmothers (abuelitas). There would be no new life without our ancestors. After that, Chac lifted a heavy piece of wood toward the spiraling sky and turned to face the four directions, at each turn whispering prayers that gave me goosebumps.

After his prayers, the muscular eagle man came closer to me and purified my body, dressed in a bikini, with the smoke of burning copal, which was the sacred incense used by the Maya in ancient ceremonies.

"Turn around," he commanded as the smoke readied my body to burn.

Chac led us from the fireplace toward the hut through the short pathway decorated with white-yellow-red flower petals.

"Welcome to the womb of Mother Nature," he said. "That womb is the connection between dying and being born again," he continued.

Life grabbed Death's hand, emphasizing their loving union.

Dusk was falling as Love, Life, Death, Freedom, and I walked toward the womb, kneeled, kissed the earth, and asked Mother Nature for permission to enter. We continued walking inside the womb in a clockwise direction and sat on the ground in a circle with rattles in our hands.

"Bienvenidas, abuelitas," Chac welcomed the incandescent volcanic rocks which the eagle man ceremonially carried into the middle of our circle inside the hut. "Everything always begins with them," Chac said and poured water mixed with sage over the hot rocks.

The water evaporated into steam and started the cleansing process. The burning sensation moved on the surface of my sweaty skin, almost like a sharp knife, from my legs toward my ears. Hot steam entered my lungs and circulated inside me, turning my upside-down tree of airways into ashes. My wet hair resting on my shoulders resembled thousands of little razor blades, which mercilessly punished my body for its every movement.

"I can't," I whispered to myself and clenched my fists.

Love gulped slowly and energetically shook a rattle with her eyes closed.

"Bienvenidas, bienvenidas, bienvenidas abuelitas," Freedom started to chant as the eagle man brought more volcanic rocks into the hut.

"Burn to die and breathe in to live again," Chac said powerfully. His words were followed by complete silence.

He splashed more sage water over the illuminated rocks, raising even more heat inside the tent. My body started to dissolve—no pain, no burn, no heart, no mind, no memory. As the temperature reached its peak, all physical pain melted away. But my heart still hurt the same from losing my grandma.

"I learned so much about joy, and now I'm burning here. Why doesn't that pain go away?" I whispered to Death.

"It isn't about continuing your life without any pain in your heart. It's about becoming stronger, to be happy even when carrying the heaviest heart," she replied.

I took a deep burning breath. I expected another heat wave, but it didn't come. The volcanic rocks were falling asleep again. Life kneeled in front of the exit, kissed the earth, and started to walk out of the womb. Freedom, Love, Death, and I followed. We all lay down on the ground in silence and watched the sky full of stars. After a while, I closed my eyes. While my body was cooling down, something cracked and started to melt in my burning heart. I opened my eyes and looked at my chest, feeling astonished. This heavy heart of mine was ready to stand up.

Temazcal ceremony. Puerto Escondido, Mexico. December 2019.

The Hero

"**I** wanted to go, but he didn't come," I said to Love in reply to her questioning look. I had been standing for thirty minutes on the side of the road with my surfboard. She badly wanted to continue learning how to surf and catch the bigger waves, but the best instructor she had found didn't pick us up for the morning session.

"What are we going to do now?" Love asked Freedom, becoming slightly impatient.

"Maybe you should call that missing ocean hero," Freedom looked at me and remarked sarcastically. Even if she was usually quite relaxed, she still couldn't get used to being late or—worse—stood up, which was a usual part of living in that part of the world.

"I tried. He didn't pick up," I said when suddenly a dark blue car with scratches all along its sides pulled up and parked right next to me.

"Karolina, right?" someone asked from the driver's side window.

"Right," I answered, faltering and hoping that I wasn't going to be kidnapped.

"I'm Hugo, your surf instructor. Where is your backpack?

We're going to paradise!" he said enthusiastically and got out of his car to help with my surfboard.

"Why would I need a backpack for a two-hour surf session?" I looked at him, confused.

"Not two hours. Three days! We're going to the Chacahua lagoons. You will love the waves there!" His good mood was rising. Even if he was shorter than me, the white smile shining from below his straw hat was perfectly visible. "Oh. Did we misunderstand each other?" Hugo asked after looking into my scared blue eyes.

"Apparently, but it's fine. Wait a moment. I will grab my backpack and some money," I told Hugo, completely forgetting that I was just meeting him for the first time.

"Fine? Are you insane? You must be careful and stay safe," Death insisted.

I looked back at Hugo's car. In the front passenger seat was a relaxed friend of his with a Hawaiian shirt draped over his shoulder, and in the back were two blonde Scandinavian-looking girls with fair skin with the surfboards in the trunk behind them.

"Well, no risk, no fun," I said to Death, and she tapped her forehead.

"Calm down; she is just trying to live in their spontaneous way," Freedom said to Death, who let out a long sigh.

"Okay, fair enough," Death said.

And after I packed a toothbrush, sunscreen, and a bit of cash, we were already on our way.

The handsome, shirtless man in the front seat introduced himself as Elio and reached his hand back to the trunk, where I was sitting together with the surfboards. The two girls looked first at his chocolate eyes framed by long, upturned lashes, then at the outstretched arm, and then quietly said something to each other in their own language.

Tranquilas, love is only for heroes. I'm not getting in your way, I thought to myself as I looked at the girls, then turned around, put my dirty feet on the back window, and sunk into music. I felt relaxed, almost as though I was in the most comfortable bed. After leaving the car in the small village called El Zapotalito and taking a boat through the mangroves and islands, we stepped onto the sandy shores of the most picturesque beach located in a national park—pristine, secluded, endless, and divine.

"Aren't those mine?" Love asked Life, who was walking next to her wearing the golden aviator sunglasses.

"Yeah, it's crazy to look at the world from your perspective." Life smiled like a teenager who had just fallen in love.

"Let me guess. You don't intend to give them back." Love rolled her eyes. "Where is your glamorous summer hat?" she asked from behind.

"I don't know. Who needs shadows when you can enjoy seeing the world through your colors?" Life answered, looking up at the sky without turning back.

"Feeling heart wants to love." Love repeated her own words, finally understanding why Life was behaving this way. She also wanted to follow her process and learn how to love.

"Look at those waves!" Hugo whistled and pointed at the ocean.

Elio grabbed his surfboard, attached the leash to his ankle, tied a portion of his semi-long chestnut hair, sun-kissed with highlights, into a bun, and started to run into water. The two girls, Hugo, and I followed, being surrounded by nothing but nature and a place to eat and sleep. After surfing, Elio sat on the beach to read a book while drinking from a coconut.

"Where are you going? Come here and chill with me," he said as I walked past on my way to take a nap in a hammock. He scooted over to make space for me on his towel.

"What are you reading?" I asked, sitting down next to him.

"*I barbari* by Alessandro Baricco," he answered.

"Read for me, please," I asked and put my head on his shoulder as if we had been friends already for a long time.

"It's in Italian," he said.

But I didn't mind. I asked him to read anyway and closed my eyes.

"Gli umani hanno una sola reale chance di diventare qualcosa di più che animali astuti: morire da eroi, e così essere consegnati alla memoria, diventare eterni, assurgere a miti. Per questo l'eroismo non è per loro una possibile destinazione del vivere, ma l'unica." He read slowly, distinctly pronouncing each word. "Did you understand any of that?" he asked.

"That we must die as brave heroes to be remembered?" I answered, recognizing only a few words. "I don't think that I would choose that. I don't think any king, warrior, or hero ever thought about everyone who was going to remember them in the moment before they died. I believe it was always love, not bravery, which brought them final peace."

Elio looked at me with curiosity and asked, "Have you already found love?"

"Yes." I looked at Love, who had recently become my close friend. That friendship was changing me—the warrior who surrendered to love was becoming a hero.

Even if my answer could mean anything, it didn't scare him off, and he continued the conversation.

"What did you do back in Europe?"

"I studied law, worked a lot, and traveled barefoot whenever I could," I answered.

"Sounds like me." He looked at me and squinted his eyes, surrounded by those extraordinarily long lashes.

"What do you want in life?" I sensed that he, like me, wasn't entirely happy with just a comfortable life.

"To earn enough to be secure and free in the future," he said, and I only smiled. "And you?" he asked back.

"To celebrate," I said cheerfully.

"To celebrate what?" He seemed surprised.

"Everything I was and everything I am now." I stopped for a moment to cherish my path so far.

"That's beautiful, but as a lawyer, you must want more than that," Elio said and combed his wet chestnut hair with his fingers.

"Cars, apartments, savings? No. Instead, I want to always follow my heart."

After a moment of silence, we both stood up, ran into the ocean, and dived under the growing waves. When we came back to shore, I walked toward the restaurant and unexpectedly spotted Love cleaning a big fish with a local fisherman.

"You need to remove the fins, scale it, cut the belly open, grab the entrails, pull them out..." A man with a long beard was explaining the process to Love, who listened carefully while holding a sharp knife in her hand. "And this is the best part you can eat—a raw heart," he took it out and showed it to her in his open hand. "Try it," he said.

She grasped it with her delicate fingers, put it in her mouth, looked up and down, and finally responded, "Quite tasty. It was worth a try."

The fisherman smiled.

"Hi, Love," I said.

"Hi. What happened? I know that kind of smile."

"I like him, but he can't be the one," I answered.

"Why?" Love asked while the fisherman continued preparing the fish without her.

"Because I already know that he likes the version of me from the past, the person I didn't want to become," I responded, proudly protecting my heart.

"Loving who you are instead of changing for someone else keeps your heart clear and bright, shining for the right ones who will never give up on looking for you." Love responded.

She thanked the fisherman for teaching her, wiped her knife clean, and admired the spotless metal for a moment before neatly putting it back in the drawer.

Dusk transformed the peaceful oasis into a parade of music and colors. It was December 12th, the day of the Feast of the Virgin of Guadalupe, which is celebrated in Mexico. The procession of colorfully dressed locals passed our beach-front restaurant, and we followed them into their village. On the right-hand side, women in colorful, floral-patterned blouses with their sleeves rolled up were chopping meat and preparing food in giant pots, which every stomach around observed impatiently. Right next to them, dancers, young and old, were creating happiness through the warmth of connected hands and steps moving backward and then forward, always back toward each other.

On the left-hand side, there was a long and simple building, inside of which was the altar of the Virgin of Guadalupe decorated with little flashing lights, abundant flowers, and balloons in the colors of the Mexican flag. Behind the building, another dancing crowd cheered on the musicians playing live music on the elevated wooden stage. Smells, sounds, colors, faith, joy, and touch blended into one unforgettable moment of celebration. Celebration that didn't praise achievements but honored having enough to love and enjoy life as it was right now.

"Will you dance with me?" Elio snuck up to me during the celebration.

He reached out his hand to me and looked at my short black dress printed with daisies. I gave him my hand, and he led the way into the middle of the crowd. I was standing in front of him barefoot, bare-faced, with salty hair and an open heart. I had never felt so visible in my entire life. He led me into a turn, and I made a circle with my eyes closed. The music slowed, and he gently swayed my body from side to side, confidently placing his hand on my shoulder. His nose grazed mine, and he blinked slowly, drawing invisible lines between his long eyelashes and my closed eyelids.

"Wait a minute. What about your heart?" Love asked me and paused the vibrant movements and sounds around us for a moment.

"I should stop. You're right," I agreed, and then the music resumed, and I said goodnight to his heart.

Our two hearts, which wanted different things, couldn't merge, but I was proud of both of us. Our search for love had brought us one step closer to finding peace as heroes who never gave up but believed in finding real love until the very end.

On the way to Chacahua Lagoons National Park,
Mexico. December 2019.

Guatemala

JANUARY – MARCH 2020

My Libertinaje

*O*uch! *I must be already burning in hell!* I thought as the black sand in El Paredón took no mercy on my soles under the scorching noon sun. This first memory from Guatemala left an unforgettable imprint on my skin.

After nine months of traveling, choosing a new direction became easy—I wanted to stay close to the Pacific Ocean. My perspective changed. I found my freedom and peace through belonging—not to a place, person, or vision but to an element that could never be tamed. Following the coastline instead of popular tourist routes felt like the best way to switch from discovering the world to finding a new home.

After walking a few steps back from the beach, I passed a turquoise fence that indicated my hostel. I checked in at the reception desk, then walked back along the fence toward the bar on the opposite side and climbed clumsily onto one of the high barstools. It was a struggle, even with my long giraffe legs.

"Cold coconut water?" asked a male bartender wearing yellow swim shorts with a black palm-tree print and a black bandana tied around his head.

"Yes, please," I answered.

"I'm Delmar, but friends call me Del," he introduced himself as he served me the coconut a minute later.

"Thank you. I'm Karolina. Hello, Del, my friend." I smiled at him, and we started to chat.

He was a bit shy, fiddled with his slim black mustache from time to time, and kept his shoulder-length brown hair tied in a ponytail. He lived for surfing and loving, as from this first conversation, his kind eyes revealed his big heart.

"I'm going to look around. See you later," I said to him and jumped down from the high stool.

The reception area, which was little more than a covered lean-to painted turquoise and surrounded by palms, was packed with surfboards. Behind that was an open-air structure with a roof made of dried palm leaves (palapa) under which guests relaxed in hammocks, did yoga, or worked out in bikinis and swim shorts. A long and narrow pathway between palms led to my dorm room with a view of the ocean and private guest huts to the right. The pathway continued to the facilities used by volunteers who worked at the bar, reception, and as yoga teachers. This paradise held enough power and space to constantly postpone people's plans to continue their travels elsewhere or to entirely cancel their flights back to lives they'd temporarily left behind.

Starting the next morning, the ocean and the first rays of the sun became my only alarm clock. I followed the pathway to the beach and took four deep breaths—into my stomach, heart, feet, and entire body. I felt so grateful for my imperfect but healthy lungs. In my right hand, I held a cup of warm water with turmeric, black pepper, and a few drops of lemon—a drink I'd learned to prepare in India. I drank it while watching the sun rise in peaceful silence.

After a few moments, I continued with a yoga sequence of my own creation combined with meditation to wake up my body in the most caring way. The following surf session in the ocean connected me with the world more than ever before—being close to nature felt like home, the thing I'd been longing for. Later I studied anatomy, learned Spanish, and socialized with people who came to the same paradise to find a joyful version of themselves—without shoes, urgency, or any long-term plan. I was constantly evolving the way I lived my life thanks to the new insights from my journey, which had brought me to the place where, for the first time, I wanted to stay to recreate myself and reconstruct my heart.

Then the evening came, and darkness swallowed up the peaceful vibe. Del, who also worked at the hostel, started his night shift and played loud reggaeton music for the two hours before sunset. Loud celebration wasn't an obvious part of his calm demeanor, but as the people who lived in the nearby village kept saying, "Nights can make anyone wild."

That saying became especially dangerous for those who escaped to paradise to forget something, to feel invincible away from their predictable lives, or to process an accumulated number of things that had become too much for their hearts to handle. My journey was powerful, but sometimes my learning was too fast and intense. It taught me how to find extraordinary strength and how to transform my life, but it didn't give my healing heart enough time to process constantly changing feelings, perspectives, and impulses.

"How do you feel living without big responsibilities and doing only what you want every day?" Del asked me as I was sitting at the bar again, drinking iced tamarind juice. He didn't ask many questions, but the ones he did always reminded me to check on my heart.

"It feels amazing right now, but it's confusing sometimes," I answered.

"Confusing?" Del asked, surprised.

"This kind of lifestyle is a big privilege, but it can also be tricky. I can't rest without worrying about wasting time. I always need to know what I want and constantly feel pressured to grow my inner drive. I also have to feel confident about my future, as I'm using all my savings right now." Del listened to me carefully as he prepared three tequila shots behind the bar. "It's also difficult to keep a healthy routine and create long-term relationships," I said as I watched his busy hands. "It's so important to enjoy it, but at the same time, I can't let myself get too used to it. Happiness shouldn't be wholly dependent on losing oneself in a fragile freedom like that," I continued.

Del placed two tequila shots with lemon and salt right next to my hand. "May it last as long as it's good for your heart!" He raised his shot to me and made me drink double with his shy but cheeky smile.

After one last swim in the salty water and watching the beautiful sunset on the beach, people followed the most powerful night current—from the bar to the dancefloor. The rhythmic Latin music moved their hips from side to side and brought them closer toward each other. When they found their favorite dancers after circling around a couple of times, they symbolically interlocked their fingers and celebrated their temporary union until the first sunlight crept over the horizon. Those who didn't find anyone raised their hands up to the starry sky and celebrated by themselves, singing as loudly as they could. I was one of those with hands upraised. After hours of dancing, I brought my hands back down and floated through the crowd of people back to the bar.

"Another drink?" Del asked as I perched on a barstool.

"Sure," I agreed. Even if I shouldn't, the dark thought of letting go of all wisdom and control made me irrationally excited for a moment.

He mixed rum with coconut water, added ice, and garnished

it with lime and mint. "Here you go. Now you can tell me about your big journey."

So I told him about the last few months and how they'd completely changed my life.

"I love the way you danced." A strange woman who was dressed up fancy with brown hair and big, gold hoop earrings suddenly sat next to me and interrupted my story, gently touching my hand.

Del smiled at her and leaned over the bar to kiss her on the cheek.

"Are you ready to party?" she asked him, looking at me as well.

"Yes, almost done," Del said and started to quickly clean around the bar.

"I'm taking her with us. Come to my house whenever you can," she said to Del, took my hand, and walked toward her brand-new black Jeep.

I opened the car door, removed a tequila bottle from my seat, and sat next to this woman who had never introduced herself. I was wearing a blue bikini and jeans shorts, without my wallet, phone, or any clue where we were going.

"This is how you want to speed up processing changes in your life?" Death asked me skeptically before getting into the car.

"Geez, stop it! Let me have some fun," I answered and slammed the car door shut.

Freedom was already sitting in the backseat, wearing her orange zebra print bikini and white boho cover-up. "Interesting way of enjoying your freedom," she remarked but didn't protest. "Please drive," she said to the strange woman, almost like a diva.

"Where are Love and Life?" I turned back and asked Death.

"They weren't feeling the crazy vibe and went to bed," she answered and yawned herself.

The woman drove fast. She seemed to know every road well, even while tipsy. I looked behind and spotted Del following in a car behind us. He bobbed his head to the rhythm of the wildly loud music from our Jeep and laughed. Feeling like I was the only one who couldn't relax, I took the bottle of tequila by my feet and opened it. *Okay, whatever. Let's go wild,* I thought to myself while sweet tequila burned my tongue.

Suddenly, the woman slowed down, took a turn, raised two fingers off the steering wheel, and waved at the guard at the security gate. We'd arrived at her enormous villa. She parked in front and switched off the car. Without the loud music blaring from the car speakers, we could hear all the sounds of celebration coming from her house—screaming, singing, boosted bass, and breaking glass. When we walked in, all the people, either naked or dressed in white, looked at her and cheered, "Long live the queen of crazy nights!"

Del parked next to her car and followed us through the house toward the impressive garden with colorful tropical plants. When we arrived at the pool, Del stripped down to his underwear and jumped right in as if he had come back to his own home. He must have known the woman and this place well. After a few moments, he beckoned me to join him with an inviting wave. Before I could walk toward him, the woman stopped me and opened her perfectly manicured hand to offer a white pill.

"Thank you, but I'm fine," I answered carefully. "Of course, we can always dance, but why not to fly?" she asked provocatively.

"I don't even know where I am or how to get back home. Not to mention your name." Nevertheless, I laughed and liked her with her mysterious darkness.

She brought her hand closer to my mouth. More suddenly than reason could explain, I spontaneously changed my mind and took the pill with my lips. I knew that being brave could be dangerous as well, but this time I didn't care. Right after I swallowed the pill, she kissed me passionately. I pretended that nothing had happened and continued walking toward Del, who was now talking to a naked girl in the swimming pool. I jumped into the water with my clothes on.

"White or naked—you're breaking the rule!" Del said, turning toward me and coming closer.

"Not only this one." I winked at him. "Are you free or taken?" I joked flirtatiously, looking at the naked girl behind him.

He laughed. I could ruin our future friendship in one night.

Before he answered, a warm euphoric sensation started rising in my body. I could suddenly feel every tiny individual water particle on my skin. It confused me.

"Are you okay?" Del touched my arm, and I felt as if his touch melted into my body.

"Can I hug you?" I asked, feeling immensely loved as a human being—by myself, the water, the world, and him.

He hugged me, sighed, and asked, "What did she give you?"

"I don't know. I don't know anything anymore. I don't even know her name," I answered in a panicked voice. I was so close to finding home in this dream place, yet I'd gotten so lost right before finally making it there.

"It has been quite a journey for you. It's okay to feel lost and overwhelmed."

He removed my messy, wet hair from my face, and I followed him out of the pool.

"You don't need to go through life bravely like a hero, managing everything in your heart all at once. No matter how hard you try, sometimes things require more attention and time," Del said.

He grabbed a random pair of men's swim shorts, green with pink flamingos, and a white linen shirt, which somebody had left at the poolside, and asked me to change in the bathroom. He was right. My journey wasn't only about becoming stronger and constantly growing but also allowing myself to slow down, process, and feel in the most human way.

"The party is over. Let's go home," Del said and led the way out of the house. I must have lost all sense of time; the whole night felt like a single minute.

In the car, Del played cheerful music, and Death fell asleep on Freedom's shoulder.

"What was that all about?" Freedom asked me from the backseat on the way back to the hostel, still gracefully sipping her orange juice with prosecco.

"You either wear white clothes or party naked," I answered, looking at the blurry road.

"No. I mean you and your crazy mode." Her tone was dead serious.

I turned around but couldn't stop imagining the orange zebra from her bikini moving and becoming alive.

"I'm sorry for abusing you. It was my moment of *libertinaje*," I answered, hoping that the sophisticated Spanish word would convince her that I still did my best to learn, especially from my mistakes. "I misunderstood why you always insist on having limitations," I tried to explain, slurring my words like a drunk.

"They are important because you aren't supposed to go through life with ease but with balance and peace," she said to me like she was explaining something to a child for the thousandth time.

When we arrived back at the hostel, I bade Del a quick goodnight and retreated back to my room.

"I'm sorry. I'm truly sorry. I promise to do better from now on. Can we go to sleep now?" I asked Freedom, who was standing next to my bed, still looking stern.

"Fine. Goodnight." She looked at me as I was holding the pair of too-big flamingo-print swim shorts at my waist. She shook her head, turned around, and tried to hide her laugh.

The Queen's Land

"¡Dios mío! There is an unconscious man lying on the sand!"

The realization immediately alarmed me as I was resting on the beach one afternoon after I had been in the village for five weeks. I ran toward the prone figure with my heart beating in my throat. When I found him, his eyes were closed, his muscular, dark-skinned body was washed by the waves, and a green jade necklace burned from the sun on his chest.

"Where is his soul? Is it still around?" I asked Life hurriedly as I knelt down next to him on the black sand.

"Slowly, slowly, you need to stay calm." She avoided answering, wanting me to blindly fight for her like any other human.

I checked his pulse—he was still alive.

"Help! Help! Help!" I shouted at the empty beach before sharing my breath with him and pressing his massive chest with the power of my hands and the strength of my warrior's heart.

"Let him go. He must go," Death said to me firmly, as if I was a stubborn child.

"I wasn't born to live by the rules but to save people's hearts," I answered her, panting heavily. In that powerful moment,

I realized that I was born to continue the Healer's mission and to always fight like the brave Warrior in his glory.

"Nobody will suffer by the Warrior Queen's ocean or on her land." Life placed her hand on Death's shoulder from behind and pulled her back.

"Her land? Did I miss something?" Death turned back and asked.

"It's all about to come because she has made enough space in her heart," Life said mysteriously, and the two of them looked at each other in agreement, mutually accepting this place as a part of their plan.

"I know that you're there. Come back to me! Breathe!" I desperately shouted at the unconscious man, exhaling deeper into his mouth and pressing his chest harder.

Suddenly, he coughed water out of his lungs, and I noticed all the people surrounding us.

"Quick! Bring some drinkable water and help me carry him out of the sun!" I told the men standing next to us.

We carried him back to the hostel and placed him on his side on a towel in the shade.

"Are you okay?" I sat next to him and touched his cheek with my cold hand.

"You saved my life," he said.

I silently smiled at him with tears in my eyes.

"I will leave you now. You're in good hands," I said, looking at his friends who were still watching us with their shocked eyes..

I didn't need to know more of his story. We were both about to start a new life.

The next day was my thirty-first birthday. Ever since my grandma died on her seventy-first, birthdays had never been the same. They held different meanings of a new beginning—coming to this earth, starting life anew, changing the way I see the world, or transforming into a beautiful new form after death. Life isn't linear and straightforward—it's a circle in which everything could happen at any time, so I learned to celebrate whatever comes.

I woke up with the sunrise and walked to the beach to greet the ocean.

"Finally!" Love said to me as we sat in a meditation position.

She had observed me for the last five weeks as I allowed myself to completely rest without learning, moving from one place to another, planning, or trying. I slowed down and followed what I learned from the dark night of grief and earlier from my beast—to be kind, understanding, and forgiving toward myself, my body, and my own heart. Slowing down was good not only for processing feelings and resting but also for reconnecting with the world and simply making new friends.

One of them, Nylia, had been volunteering at the reception desk for a few months. She was taller and older than me, had long, wavy blonde hair, and spoke English with a Swiss accent. We had both left successful corporate careers to change our lives and chose practicing yoga, meditation, and surfing over wild partying. She was the first one to hug me when I walked back from the beach, wishing me "Happy birthday!"

After that, I walked to the bar and spotted Del waiting for me with a banana cake.

"This is crazy. Thank you! How did you know?" I said, coming closer and hugging him, feeling loved and surprised.

"I know and have already seen everything, my friend." He winked at me and opened two coconuts to start our day.

From my spot, I could smell that somebody was cooking my favorite Middle Eastern dish called foul. I peeked into the kitchen where Aladdin, Del's best friend from Lebanon, who worked at the hostel as a yoga teacher, was mixing mashed fava beans, chickpeas, tahini paste, crushed garlic, lemon juice, cumin, and salt.

"Del! Get her out of here. It's a surprise!" he shouted from the kitchen.

While many girls had burned their hearts in the past weeks obsessing over his yoga teaching, handsome tattooed body, and dark shoulder-length curls, he had become one of my most loving friends.

After an hour of chatting with Del about the places where he caught the best waves in his life, Aladdin shouted from the kitchen, "I'm ready!"

People from the hostel surrounded me and started to sing 'Happy birthday.' I blushed. Del laughed at me as he had never seen me so shy. Nylia clapped her hands, looking as happy as if it was her own celebration.

Aladdin served foul with flatbread, grilled vegetables, and fresh tomatoes mixed with parsley. He kissed me on the top of my head and said, "Happy birthday, our amazing girl."

He sat next to me at the table, and before he could say something more, I took his still dirty hands into mine and kissed them.

"Thank you for loving and caring so much," I said.

And he smiled.

Becoming a family in the village wasn't a birthright but people's choice. I felt so privileged to be chosen by the people I loved so much after knowing them only for such a short time. Even though there was no supermarket, shopping mall, fancy restaurant, or cinema nearby, people had everything they ever needed—they became that for each other. And together with the Pacific Ocean, they became everything I needed to feel at home.

"How about going for a walk on the beach?" Nylia asked me after she'd finished her work at the reception desk and changed her loose leopard-print shirt for a wine-red crocheted tank top.

"Sure, let's go," I answered. I grabbed my green cup with yerba mate and stepped onto the black sand, which didn't burn my feet as much as before.

"What is your birthday wish or dream that you want to follow?" Nylia asked after we'd walked for a bit. Dreams fascinated her almost as much as surfing.

"Eventually, I would like to build my ocean resort, a home where I could help people to connect with, transform, or rescue their hearts." I tried to put words to my newborn dream for the first time as I looked at peacefully swaying palms along the beach.

"Why not do it here?" Nylia pointed to a spot we were passing by behind the palms, an empty piece of land with nothing but dried grass.

"You mean to start building it here? Now?" I looked at the lifeless and sunbaked land.

"I love this idea. I think that we should stay in the village and try." She wiggled her toes in the sand with excitement as the refreshing waves washed over her feet. "Don't you feel at home here?" She looked at me with encouraging eyes.

I felt that something had changed inside me. Even if my mind quickly pointed out the unrealistic probability of success, financial constraints, and unknowns about life in this part of the world, I didn't even try to argue against my heart. Words like 'never,' 'impossible,' and 'not the right time' had stopped existing since I learned how to combine the most powerful forces in my life—courage, hard work, and the calling of my heart.

"Are we ending our journey here?" Death asked, walking right behind us, looking happy in her red bikini and a new straw hat.

"Probably. I think that she figured out enough," Freedom answered, looking at me and nodding her head with respect.

"But what about love?" Life looked at Love, the one who might have still been disappointed. Even though I had tried hard to learn from her, I hadn't yet found the one to create my new life with.

"Loving heart wants to grow." Love repeated the last step of her healing process and happily sipped from her coconut. "Following her dreams is the highest form of loving herself, the most powerful growth I could hope for," she said, satisfied, and winked at Life as if she was forming another secret plan.

Let's do this! I decided then. I turned my head back and nodded at Love, Life, Death, and Freedom walking next to each other. Then I looked again at Nylia with a confident smile and repeated the same aloud. I was no longer the wandering Warrior Queen but Queen of the Coast and ruler of my own life.

El Paredón, Guatemala. March 2020.

You reached the end of my memoir.
See the continuation of my life story on social media.
@moleculeofhappiness

MOLECULEOFHAPPINESS

***

What you think and feel is important.
Expressing it can change your and others' lives.

If you have a moment, please write a book review.
It will help me to reach more people
who could learn from my story.

Thank you.

Thank you to...

Love for teaching me how to trust and take care of my heart,

Life for making me the best version of myself,

Death for teaching me how to accept the unacceptable,

Freedom for teaching me how to allow myself to be happy;

my mom, Edyta, for showing me how to be brave, grow, and heal myself as well as others,

my dad, Jan, for teaching me how to fight, forgive, and unconditionally love, regardless of everything that kept us apart,

my sister, Malwina, for being the Yin to my Yang and the sunshine in my entire life journey,

myself for caring about the world above everything and working hard to share this story;

and all friends and almost strangers around the world who supported me in the making of this book.

I love you.